T0163963

JUST THIS SIDE OF NORMAL

Glimpses Into Life with Autism

Elizabeth King Gerlach

FUTURE HORIZONS INC.
Arlington, Texas

FUTURE HORIZONS INC.

721 W. Abram Street, Arlington, Texas 76013
817-277-0727
800-489-0727
817-277-2270 (Fax)
E-mail: info@FHautism.com
www.FHautism.com

© 1999 by Elizabeth King Gerlach

AUTHOR'S NOTE: Many of the names of family
and friends have been changed.

Printed in the United States of America

ISBN 10: 1-932565-03-5
ISBN 13: 978-1-932565-03-4

For Cyndi

Acknowledgments

Jane Novick, my friend and editor, has now guided me through two books. She has given so much of her time and expertise that I cannot begin to thank her. Without her long-standing love and support I doubt that I would be an author.

There are so many people to thank and so little space! Thanks to Karen Esperanza, Julie Cherry, Steve Edelson, Jane Taylor McDonnell, Marguerite Kelly, Elizabeth Lyon, Joan Cookson, Christine and Solala Towler, Jennifer Wright, and Rand Gerlach. Everything came together, thanks to their help.

I'm grateful to Jean Yates for the humor, the wit, and inspiration she supplies on a daily basis.

Jeff Strong and Beth Kaplan were particularly helpful in encouraging me to see the bigger picture as well as tend to the fine details. Many thanks to my family: Jane and Ken Austin, the Kings, Vivian and Fred McNeil, and my Aunt Marilyn.

I love and appreciate Nick, who is a great teacher to me. Finally, I want to thank my son Ben, for his presence and for his bright giving.

Introduction

"When I grow up I want to be a screwdriver!" My six-year-old is spinning outside his school in front of the teacher's lounge, where through the windows I can see the staff drinking sodas and looking at us through the corners of their eyes. His eyes are closed as he spins.

I've been called to the school (yet again) to help my son regain his composure, and although I'm about to lose mine, his choice of future employment fascinates me.

"Why a screwdriver?" I ask him.

"Because they go round and round, Mom, like a whirlpool, like a tornado, like this." He starts to spin. He loves to spin. I watch him spin down the sidewalk.

Why does he spin? Somehow I think it boils down to the reason most humans do almost anything.

1

Ultimately, it makes him feel good.

Of course, the earth is spinning as I write this, so, in a sense, every moment that we live and breathe we do so spinning. When water goes down the drain, it spins. In fact, spinning occurs regularly in nature. Yet spinning is not something most of us do frequently—unless we like to get dizzy and fall down, or are a Whirling Dervish and connect with God this way, or perhaps have autism. My son falls in the latter category. At any rate, it comforts me to know that the world is spinning at this very moment. I'm always looking for tie-ins to the greater reality.

A memory comes to me . . . I was twelve years old and watched a TV special on autism. I saw a little boy rocking in a corner and another little boy spinning plates, each oblivious to the world around him. After watching that show I picked up my cat, walked outside, and cuddled him to me. I was shocked to learn that there were children like that. I looked up at the trees and then to the sky, thinking to myself, "Autism must be the hardest thing a parent could face."

Now, having lived with autism for twelve years, in many ways I still believe this to be true. However,

I have learned that autism is not always as obvious as a child rocking or spinning plates in a world of his or her own. Autism can present itself in a variety of ways: inconsolable tantrums, a preference for playing alone, eyes that look through you. . . .

Autism is a profound, engulfing disability that affects brain function. It impairs a person's sensory processing system, affecting their ability to communicate and to relate to the world the way the majority of us do. Autism is often accompanied by other disorders, such as developmental delay and epilepsy. There is no test for it. One watches with growing apprehension as one's child develops differently from other children. Or one watches their precious child lose whatever language and social skills had previously been gained. At this writing, the cause is still unclear, a cure still a wish.

Parents of children with autism today face a myriad of treatment choices, none of which guarantees improvement. Intensive behavioral and educational intervention, vitamin therapy, diet modifications, and medications are among the many, many possible options. Each individual with autism is so unique that what alleviates symptoms in one person might well do nothing for another.

Experimental treatments appear regularly. I was so confused by the many choices I discovered while trying to help my son, Nicky, I was compelled to write my first book, *Autism Treatment Guide*, in the hope of helping others.

As a young mother, I was not prepared to have a child with a disability. Most of us dread the thought of seeing our own child suffer. We also fear that we would be unable to cope and that our personal dreams would be shattered.

Society views disability as a "tragedy." In fact, the greater tragedy is society's larger and erroneous view that there is such a state as "normal." This view, in itself, sometimes feels like a greater burden than the disability.

"Normal" does exist, but you have to look for it. It is a place that is somewhere between the middle of two extremes. For instance, there are shampoos for oily, normal, or dry hair. Another good example of normal can be found on my clothes dryer, between "fluff" and "shrink it." This area is marked "normal." I use this setting frequently because it is the closest to normal my life usually gets.

The truth is, "normal" is not a word that should

apply to the human condition. People are different, and they constantly change. A close approximation to "normal" might be "balanced." For example, the body will work overtime to fight an infection and return to a healthful state. Balance is a state of being we often strive for—a sort of happy comfortableness. And some of us endeavor to maintain a balanced state within ourselves, our families, and our communities. We have to discover what this means for ourselves, and this too changes over time.

Mothering a child who is "different" has given me an opportunity to think a lot about all this. It has been a process that has caused me to look within and has frequently challenged me to change my beliefs.

I used to think there was such a thing as a "normal, happy family" and that it was something attainable. I hadn't experienced that as a child, so I set out to create it as an adult. Autism bombed that notion. Just as well. I'm not pretending that autism, in its varying degrees of severity, isn't painful in many ways for everyone involved. It is. I'm simply saying that some of that pain is relieved with understanding and acceptance. Having a child with a disability has shown me how precious life really is and that being human means learning to love. The simplicity and complexity of this understanding never cease to amaze me.

The vignettes that follow are glimpses into the twelve years that I have shared so far with my son. This book does not presume to describe all there is about living with autism or any other disability. It is offered as an expression of gratitude for my life despite it all.

Living minute to minute, hour to hour, day after day, is the human condition, and it is rarely glamorous. But we are all granted moments when clarity shines through, moments of grace. They are cool drinks of well water that sustain us. They are sweeter when shared.

—*Elizabeth K. Gerlach*

Chapter 1

My son's first year started off uneventfully. During his second year, Nicky started to "slip away" from us slowly, the way colors fade at twilight. Just as nightfall wipes away color and texture, leaving only silhouettes and bare forms, autism seemed to obscure my beautiful child and hide him away in darkness.

Nicky at Eighteen Months

A small body in overalls falls to the floor. His thrashing breaks open the snaps at the crotch. A head with its baby-fine blond hair hits the wooden floor and bounces up like a ball. His eyes seem glazed. They do not connect. He does not respond to words of comfort.

Is he hungry? Is he sick? Is he jealous of his baby brother? Are the terrible twos coming early? Like

Rumplestiltskin, will he break a hole right through the floor?

When I pick him up to console him he arches backwards, pushing me away with his angry fists, and slides out of my arms. His small body takes on the force of a hot wind.

Nicky at 20 Months

The doctor's office is in a grand old house that has been converted into several offices. She is a wonderful doctor, and because of this there is always a long wait for an appointment. When that day arrives, almost inevitably there is a long wait in the foyer.

Nicky moves from the Little People farm to the race car station to the wooden blocks, all in about three minutes. Then he takes off to explore the rest of the place. I have to chase him down the stairs, fearfully leaving Ben, only three months old, and herd Nicky back to the sagging couch.

"Let's read *Pat the Bunny*," I say. This holds his attention for a good two minutes. Round two, three, and four and . . . could it be that they are running thirty minutes behind?

Finally, the assistant calls my name. I hoist the baby chair and balance it on my hip. I almost grab Nicky's hand before he dashes into the blood-work lab, but he is too fast for me. Eventually, we all make our way up a flight of stairs and into the examining room. We wait another twenty minutes. Nicky is absorbed in the shiny trash can with its lid that flips up and down, up and down. He throws Gumbie and Pokey around the room. Luckily, I brought snacks.

Our pediatrician is warm and kind. I tell her that Nicky is starting to throw a lot of fits. She checks his ears. He has had chronic ear infections since he was nine months old, but after tubes were put in at thirteen months this condition has improved. Today we are here for a recheck.

I tell her that I am worried that he isn't putting words together, and that sometimes I have trouble getting his attention.

He grabs at her shiny stethoscope and tries to taste it.

"What a big, curious boy you are!" She pats him on the belly and he recoils giggling. "You are as busy as you can be! Healthy too. Don't give your mom too much trouble." She turns and smiles reassuringly at me. "Children develop at different rates, Elizabeth.

Don't worry so much."

Her exam takes about four minutes. She gives him a happy face sticker. I write a check for a clean bill of health.

Nicky at Two

The spacious, sunny room is a kid's paradise, complete with giant wooden blocks, big red cardboard bricks, plastic slides, and an art easel. There is a birdseed table, where children pour grains through funnels into bottles and dump them out again.

"Have fun with your toddler in an enriching, creative environment." The description of the "Definitely Two" class every Tuesday and Thursday at the Community Center sounded so inviting, so positive. It's supposed to be a time to interact with other parents and kids, and Nicky's a little over two. I sign us up. My husband, Rand, offers to come home for lunch during class time to watch Ben.

Today is our third class. Nicky is pouring little grains of millet from one cup to another. Back and forth, back and forth. The teacher calls everyone to circle time, and children amble over to sit on bright carpet squares. All except Nicky, who resists leaving the table. When I insist that we move to the circle, he hurls birdseed into the air and runs away. With a red face I search for the broom.

"Zoom, zoom, zoom, we're going to the moon." The other children sit with their mom or dad and sing along with the teacher. Meanwhile, Nicky literally zooms around the room. I catch him, carry him to the circle, and hold him firmly on my lap. We manage to "blast-off" together with the others, but then he tries to squirm out of my lap. I grip him tightly. Luckily, "I'm a Little Teapot" is next. He likes this one and sings along. At the end, he tips his body sideways and then dramatically crashes to the ground.

"You've got an active one!" I have heard this remark from a number of parents, not just here, but at the park, at day care. . . . I imagine that what they are really thinking is, "Why can't you control your child?" The truth is, I don't know whether I should be patient or stern. Neither approach seems to affect him much. Maybe he is hyperactive or just has a lot of energy. I wish he would slow down and enjoy the group activities like the other children. He prefers to play on his own, often lining things up, knocking them apart, and lining them up again. It bothers me that I've started to dread coming to what I thought would be a fun experience for us.

It's time to go. Nicky runs around and throws himself on a pile of cardboard bricks. I struggle with him to get his coat on. The teacher says brightly, "Bye, bye, Nicky," but he runs past her, out the door, without a glance.

Nicky at Two and a Half

"What is your name?" asks the operator standing by on the other end of the line. I have called the "Parent Crisis Hotline," a number I've seen on TV. In a shaky voice I say, "I just wanted some help. I'm calling because I feel like hitting my child and I don't want to. He's been screaming for over an hour and he won't calm down."

"May I have your name, please?" she repeats. Why? What would that mean? Would someone come and take my child away? Fear rolls inward. I feel my stomach muscles tighten. I do not answer her, and I carefully place the receiver back on the phone.

The tantrums, like storm clouds, loom darkly. Fear of them dictates when and where I dare to go.

I avoid taking Nicky to any stores—I hate the stares of strangers. The tantrums are unpredictable, sharp earthquakes that rattle my world and leave broken bits of self-esteem to clean up afterwards.

I have asked friends and family what to do, but no one seems to understand. All I hear is, "It's the terrible twos, terrible twos." But the growing frequency of his outbursts leaves me feeling helpless and vulnerable. I am feeling angry more often.

Over the last few weeks I've tried everything—reprimands, time-outs—all in a firm, loving manner. I have read up on parenting. I had hoped I'd never have to spank either one of my kids. But I try that too, for lack of other ideas. Even that seems to have no effect, as if pain does not register with Nicky.

The screams from the other room invade every cell of my body. All attempts to calm him have failed. I am a failure. Who can I turn to? I look blankly at the telephone.

My son is pulling hard on his door. The door is held shut by a stiff piece of twine that is tied to the knob of the door across the hall. A friend suggested that I lock him in his room after hearing me complain bitterly that he is unresponsive to other attempts at control. "Unthinkable!" I told her, but that was two weeks ago. Today, when he rushed at me full of rage and clawed at me, I felt that I could strike him; I felt my heart turn in a cold direction. Something in me was ready to snap, but I would hurt myself before I would hurt him.

I walk into the hallway and sink down to the floor beside the door. "Please calm down, Honey," I beg. My own childhood memories of misguided discipline swirl around me like demons, taunting me, torturing me. I hear a child crying. But the child is myself, cowering in the corner away from an all too familiar belt in the hand of my out-of-control parent. I tell myself I must, MUST, break that chain.

The screams give way to the sound of toys hitting the wall. Is the yellow school bus flying? In the nursery, the baby starts to cry; I must tend to him. Trembling, I peer into his crib. He smiles at me . . . why doesn't Nicky ever smile? I carry Ben outside to the front porch and feed him. The screams eventually subside.

Nicky has cried himself to sleep. Anxious to see if he is all right, I put the baby in his playpen. He bats at the colorful mobile clipped on the side, and I wind it up so it will play "Mary Had a Little Lamb."

The twine has been cinched so tightly to the doorknob from Nicky's pulling that I must cut it with scissors to open the door. The unmistakable smell of excrement insults me as I enter the room. I see it smeared on the wall across from me. Tears stain Nicky's face, which looks peaceful now. I cover him with the blanket I made for him when he was born. Blankie. I glance around the room, strewn with toys, and go to fetch paper towels and cleaner.

Horrified, I erase the mess on the wall, clean his hands, and go to the bathroom to wash my own hands and face. I want to wash this nightmare and all of my anger and doubt away. I tiptoe back into his room and stroke his hair, careful not to wake him. He looks so angelic now. I wonder, why can't I seem to cope? I've always wanted to be a mother, a good mother. Why is it so hard? It must be me. Something is wrong with me.

Nicky at Three
I take Nicky to the community center for an Easter Egg hunt. The hunt has not quite begun. I try to ex-

plain that there is candy inside some eggs and that he is supposed to find them. Of course, he can't see any eggs because they are hidden, and therefore he doesn't understand at all and is starting to become agitated. We stand in the middle of a mown field amid all the children dressed in fresh spring clothes. They race around with their bright baskets. There is noise and chaos as the kids wait for the "Go!"

Nicky takes one look at the person approaching who is dressed as a gargantuan Peter Cottontail and falls screaming to the ground, a glazed look coming over his eyes. He cannot be calmed. Parents are videotaping their little ones. I wonder if someone on the edge of their screen captures the image of me dragging my screaming child back to the car, buckling him in, and slamming the door against his wails.

I look back at all the happy children and feel so alienated. Why doesn't my child want what other children want? Why isn't he greedily looking for hot, sticky jellybeans and melted chocolate robin's eggs? Why can't we share this special holiday happily, like everybody else? Why, why, why?

But in my heart I know why. Over the last year and a half Nicky has become increasingly hard to manage. It was next to impossible to find a new preschool for him because at three years of age he still is not potty trained. When we did find one, he cried in a corner most of the mornings. I finally removed him because I couldn't bear to think of him as being so miserable.

At our final meeting, the teacher commented that Nicky didn't seem to hear her, and so we took him to a hearing specialist. The specialist found nothing wrong with his hearing, but thought it curious that he seemed to look through her and that when he fell and hit his head, he didn't cry.

"Is he always so insensitive to pain?" she asked. She suggested that we have him tested further. When I asked her what she suspected, she said a word that nearly killed me: autism.

We are waiting to have him "officially" diagnosed.

After taking Nicky home from the egg hunt, I go for a walk along the river. The bridge there offers a vista, a place to clear my mind of disappointment—a place to take deep breaths. Looking down, I am startled to see two eggs clinging between rocks and river grass in the middle of the current. I stare at them a long time, marveling at the odds of their surviving in that harsh place. I am happy that I am here on Easter to see them. I hear the rushing of the river and feel the rushing of days. I cherish this moment of faith.

Nicky at Four

Today Nicky will receive his second diagnosis. The first psychiatrist we saw had never diagnosed a case of autism. A friend suggested we get a second opinion from a team of specialists at the University. This will be a grueling five-hour day of assessments.

Yesterday I went to my chiropractor to get myself "balanced," but that was wishful thinking. I could not sleep last night and lay awake with a knot in my stomach.

"They are going to diagnose my child with an incurable brain disorder" is all I can think of as I brush my teeth. Good thing I'm in the bathroom. Nausea overtakes me. Diarrhea immediately follows. We have waited six months for this appointment and I can't believe I'm sick. Rand takes Nicky alone while I go to my doctor's office and sob to her that I need something to get me through this appointment.

I manage to make it to the University only an hour late. I walk through the door next to the sign that says "Crippled Children's Service Division." I want to burst into tears again, but I bite the inside of my cheek and find the right room.

The speech and language specialist, clipboard in hand, talks to our son, who seems oblivious to her. Through the one way mirror, Rand and I observe him talking into a toy telephone. "No lettuce and chop the pickle. No lettuce and chop the pickle. No lettuce and chop the pickle," he repeats over and over, ignoring the therapist's questions. I recognize this from a *Yogi Bear* video.

Rand and I, ushered into a stark office, answer a battery of questions from a psychologist. "No, I did not drink or take drugs while I was pregnant. I don't think he showed a reaction to any vaccinations. The pregnancy and birth seemed normal. Is there a history of this in my family? I'm not sure."

I try to remember that these questions might somehow help researchers uncover similarities, help with the bigger picture, but right now I feel as though my private life is being invaded. I'm glad when the questions are finished.

We take Nicky into the pediatrician's room. Again we are asked many questions, often similar to those that the psychologist had just asked. I feel inadequate when I can't remember the precise day he walked or exactly when the tantrums began. I wish I had written it all down in a notebook or something. While we are trying to concentrate on questions and answers, Nicky tries to get into all the drawers and make the table go up and down.

We are shown into a social worker's office while they take Nicky for more observation. We stare at the social worker blankly when he asks us how we are feeling. I think "exhausted" would be the word.

We all assemble in a large conference room, Rand, Nicky, and I and four professionals. Nicky is still on a roll; he climbs on the table and chairs and attempts to scale the bookcase.

"We unanimously feel that your child fits the criteria for a diagnosis of autism."

A lump rises in my throat, but there are no tears. There is no time for tears at the moment. Nicky crashes backwards in the chair he was climbing on, taking a few thick books with him. We compose ourselves and somehow walk out of there, our fate freshly labeled but not sealed.

Chapter 2

"Evening star, you bring all things which the bright dawn has scattered: you bring the sheep, you bring the goat, you bring the child back to its mother." (Sappho)

Nicky at Four and a Half

Carrie counts the money in the cash box and sips Diet Pepsi from the quart-size plastic mug that is never far from her side. She is the main secretary at Rand's office, and a crackerjack organizer. "Move that sign to the front of the table so everyone can see it," she chirps to one of her nieces, one of the many people on call to help. "Proceeds from this sale go to the Nicky Gerlach Fund," it reads. Here in the basement of Rand's office, the "garage" sale begins.

Two men dressed in plaid shirts hoist a sofa down

the concrete stairs. An old dishwasher, practically an antique, is rolled in from the door adjoining the alley. We unload boxes and boxes filled with coffee pots, candlesticks, toys, clothes, and disco albums. Someone from accounting, I think, prices everything with brightly colored sticky dots. Several kids have sticky dots covering their faces and beg chocolate chip cookies from the bake sale table. I eye a vintage blue wool peacoat.

It is the culmination of a fundraiser begun about six weeks ago. Jean, one of Rand's associates, got wind of the cost of the specialized educational program we have chosen as a way to help Nicky. The cost of the one-week session is high, not to mention traveling across the country to receive it.

Jean wasted no time. An account was set up at a local bank, and throughout last month and this, Rand's co-workers have donated money directly from their paychecks to this fund. An article in the local newspaper generated even more donations. Last week, the Park District, which employs Rand, gave all the proceeds from an evening's attendance at the indoor pool to the Nicky Gerlach Fund.

When Rand first told me about the fund I thought, "Great, we're a charity case!" Rand, also proud, protested to Jean, but it was too late. The ball was already rolling. Our mixed emotions were soon allayed when we discovered how much people wanted to do this. It reminded me of how, when I was a child and got stranded barefoot in a patch of prickers, my grandfather rescued me with a piggy-back ride. These friends are doing the same—helping us over a rough spot.

By the end of the day only a few items remain. I brush brownie crumbs off the table and help box up what is left over. Mitch, the person in charge of grounds maintenance, comes up and grabs my hand.

"This whole thing has brought all the employees together. I can't remember anything since I've worked here that has felt so rewarding. I know a lot of people feel this way. It's a gift for us too."

I am so overcome with emotion that I must excuse myself. I go to the bathroom and cry silently in the stall. Life has been upside down for us since Nicky's autism took over. There have been times when we have felt utterly alone and fearful of the future. But this outpouring of time, energy, and generosity has given us a sense that we aren't really alone. *Now Mitch tells me it is a gift to them too.*

I wash my face and return to the sales table. I put $5.00 in the jar and stash the unsold peacoat under the table. "Elizabeth, don't you think that is a little absurd? After all, the money is going to you!" Carrie ribs me good naturedly. I just wink and smile. At the last minute, unbelievably, someone buys the dishwasher.

Nicky at Five

My Aunt Marilyn calls me from Texas to tell me about an article she read in *The Reader's Digest* about a girl who practically recovered from autism after receiving a certain kind of therapy called auditory integration training. I call the office of *The Reader's Digest*, desperately trying to find out where Nicky can receive this new technique. The receptionist sighs loudly. . . . Obviously I am not the first Desperate Mother who has called. She can't tell me anything, but asks if I'd like to subscribe.

I hang up from the dead-end call and start to pace. Who should I call next? Finding help for Nicky is like a tidal wave that some days I ride but which other days sucks me under. All I know is that I keep coming up for air and keep treading water, all the time waiting for a lifeboat.

I call one of the case workers whom I haven't seen much of since we took Nicky out of preschool last year. Had she read the article? Does she have any information? She says she will get on the phone and ask around. She reports back that the only scientific study of this therapy being conducted in the country is near Portland, Oregon, less than one hundred miles from my home!

The training is especially suited for children who show hearing sensitivity. Nicky often runs screaming, hands over his ears, when he sees a bus coming because of the screech of the brakes. When the lawn mowers crank up and split the peace of Saturday mornings, he hides under his bed. When I sing, he begs me to stop. Barking dogs make him cry.

I phone Steve Edelson, the researcher. He is kind, but early in our conversation he states dryly, "I'm having my home phone number changed tomorrow because too many parents like you have tracked me down."

"What's the new number going to be?" I shoot back. "Now that I've found you, you aren't getting rid of me that easily."

"Sorry, but the study is full, and I don't know when I'll be conducting further studies."

"Where can I go?" I ask.

"This is it, for now. No one else has been trained or is doing it. Unless you can go to France."

"France is out. Listen, we are here, in Oregon, practically family. You get a cancellation and we'll walk to this study. Please put us first on the waiting list."

"I can't promise you anything, but I'll write your name down as a back-up." Click.

Two months pass.

Someone cancels.

My mother comes up to help out. Because we think the daily drive would be too hard on Nicky, Rand and I take shifts for a total of ten days in a hotel in a tiny town twenty-five miles from Portland. For thirty minutes, morning and afternoon, Nicky listens to music through headphones. We feed him Gummi Bears at thirty-second intervals—whatever it takes to get him to sit still and listen to the music of Stevie Wonder, Bob Dylan, and others. The music is modulated through a machine, and it sounds like it is going through a blender, a washing machine, and a roller coaster simultaneously. Somehow, it might possibly alter the way his brain processes sound. This, in turn, could make the sounds of the world less painful and more meaningful, and thus help him in any number of ways. Or not. No one knows how or if it works. Propelled by hope and desperation, we plunge ahead.

It is the longest ten days of my life. We kill time at the hotel pool. A teenage boy with autism, never moving from one corner, splashes water over and over onto the side of the pool. His mother tells me her son can hear a blender in the cafeteria, which is on the other side of the school from his class.

Getting to know Dr. Edelson, I learn that he is one of the kindest and most devoted professionals I have ever met. He seems to accept all the children's "odd" behaviors without judgment, and he works hard to establish rapport with them. I also learn that Dr. Edelson's mother had suffered a serious stroke around the same time I had initially called him. He explained that he was jumpy every time the phone rang, thinking it might be news that his mother's condition had worsened.

We explore every park within a ten-mile radius. I encounter a mother and her twelve-year-old son.

She spins him on the merry-go-round. The boy looks beyond pale and moves slowly from the merry-go-round to the picnic table. His mother tells me he is recovering from chemotherapy treatments for cancer—as if autism weren't enough.

One night, near the end of the treatments, Nicky will not go to sleep. He has caught a cold, and the congestion is bothering him badly. I turn on the shower; hot steam fills the bathroom. We huddle together in this make-shift vaporizer, and it gives him a little relief. Steam escapes into the foyer and sets off the fire alarm. Mom and I stop the siren by fanning desperately with hotel towels before the manager calls to see what the trouble is.

Mom tells me to go for a walk. It is the middle of the night, and I sit out on the hotel stairs crying and wondering why all of this is even happening, and happening to me.

When I come back, Nicky is still bellowing about his stuffy nose. His honking, yelling, and snorting have been going on for three hours. We hear a sharp knock on the wall from our undoubtedly frustrated neighbors. Nicky stops his clamoring, cocks his head, and knocks back. Somehow, we make it until dawn.

At the emergency room of the nearby hospital, the only place open on Sunday, we discover that Nicky has a double ear infection. We don't know if this will affect the auditory integration training. But there is only one day to go. We finish up and go home.

It is three months later. We've been told to record anything and everything. Each week we fill out a lengthy questionnaire. There has been no miracle cure as far as we can tell, but then we aren't expecting that. (At least that is what we tell ourselves over and over.)

New neighbors move in across the street. We invite them over to get acquainted. Nicky brings a stool into the living room and says, "I'm Nicky." Three months ago he would have run screaming into his room at the sight of strangers. But here he sits, smiling.

I can hardly talk to my new neighbors. I just keep staring at Nicky in disbelief. I want them to leave so I can hug him and cry. My boy is better. For the first time in three years I feel hope.

Nicky at Five and a Half

Ships are Nicky's true love. He builds them ever so carefully, in a very particular order, with big Leggos. When they are done he looks at them proudly for about five seconds. Then he becomes a thunderstorm and crashes them. He picks up the pieces and starts over. He will do this perhaps twenty or thirty times a day.

Intensive intervention, via education or daily skill training, is thought to be one of the most effective means of helping children with autism. The training program we chose emphasized using Nicky's interests or obsessions as avenues towards connecting with him and reaching him. We try to sail into his world.

For a long while, he does not allow us to touch his ship. We can watch. Eventually we begin to build ships next to him. We make our ships more and more elaborate. We craft sails from paper and rigging from yarn. On a breakthrough day he might ask us to put a sail on his ship too. We offer to hold the paper while he cuts it. He tapes it on. His fingers don't like to move in certain ways. He sometimes winces when he cuts. Yet, he is as dexterous as a monkey with the Leggos.

Little plastic people play on our ships. "The ship must have a captain. Where are your sailors? Ships need people! People need people, Nicky!" He pretends he does not hear us. He does not need us. He sails his people-free ship in his own private ocean.

"What do you do with a drunken sailor, what do you do with a drunken sailor, what do you do with a drunken sailor, early in the morning?" I belt out this tune from childhood. Trying to get his attention, I fall on the floor and roll around. Over the weeks he learns the words, and we sing this song together. For three precious stanzas we connect.

Mary, one of his volunteer teachers, also sings a song. "Sailing on the ocean blue . . . ," she lilts. Teasingly she sings, "Sailing on the ocean purple."

"No, no, no," he rigidly insists. Yet he laughs too, and asks her to sing it one more time, with some compromise. They sing, "Sailing on the ocean blue, NOT green." Mary turns this into a game of change, small tolerable change. They sail on an ocean of blue, NOT polka dots.

Books with ships are good. *Scuppers the Sailor Dog, The Walloping Window Blind,* even *The Great Age of Sail.* He will at least look at these. We read them over and over. I spell out S-H-I-P with plastic magnetic letters. He looks at them from the corner of his eyes.

For Christmas he asks for an expensive Leggo ship with hundreds of tiny pieces. It is for ages twelve and up. He is still five. We opt to get him a ship of durable plastic, one that most children would fight for. He throws it across the room and will have nothing to do with it. He says nothing.

Six months later, out of the blue he says, "For my birthday I'd like the right ship. The Leggo ship."

We give him the Leggo ship for his birthday. Nicky needs a little help building the ship the first time. He learns how to follow the instructions. It takes him about a week to build the first ship, and five seconds to crash it. He starts over. He memorizes the plans and builds it from memory. And crashes it again.

Over time, the routines slowly change, one sail at a time. We turn his entire room into a ship and he pretends to be captain. He waits sometimes up to two weeks to crash his intricate Leggo ship. Who knows, someday he may be a captain of the high seas, sailing on the ocean blue (NOT purple).

Nicky at Six

Nicky finds peace and comfort in his green sleeping bag. He will spend upwards of an hour in it if possible. It is dark, warm, and quiet. His senses are given rest from the sounds of life.

I sit and tell him stories while he lies motionless in the bag. Perhaps I will pretend to be a bear in winter and crawl in a sleeping bag of my own. I'll come out claustrophobic and dripping with sweat.

Still he stays in there, happy to be insulated from a world where bright lights, loud sounds, and strong smells relentlessly insult his system.

He drags his sleeping bag outside in the summer, crawls in on days when the temperature soars to eighty degrees. He sleeps in it at night; he will not hear of comforters or flannel sheets. The sleeping bag travels with him, a portable, private closet.

A volunteer tells Nicky about the life cycle of butterflies.

"Look, I'm a cocoon. Safe and warm."

One day he says, "Look, I'm a chrysalis."

I grow hopeful and look up what the word means. "An intermediate, usually quiescent form assumed by metabolic insects after the larval stage, and maintained until the beginning of the adult or imaginal stage."

A toe appears.

"Nicky, will you become a butterfly?" I ask.

A little voice wavers through the fabric tunnel.

"Someday, but not yet."

Chapter 3

Sometimes we see the dew sparkling on the petals, sometimes we see the veins on the leaves, sometimes we see the whole rose.

Nicky at Six

> **Rosetta stone** (ro•zet′a). A tablet of black basalt, found in 1799 at Rosetta, a town in Egypt near the mouth of the Nile, bearing a trilingual inscription in hieroglyphics, Egyptian demotic characters, and Greek, and famous as having given M. Champollion the first clue toward deciphering the Egyptian hieroglyphics. (*Webster's Dictionary*)

Stuck in five o'clock traffic in July, without air conditioning, tempers escalate. The boys squirm in the back seat of the car. Hot and sticky, each pokes at the other or hits the other with books and toys. Who will reign as king of the backseat?

My mother rides with me in the front, and we alternate turning around to tell them, "Settle down!" or "Keep your hands to yourself!" Tired from a day at the pool and restless to get out of his seat, Nicky shows his stress by talking incessantly, his words a recitation of *Farmyard Friends*, a cassette tape he listens to frequently.

I turn on the radio, wanting to drown out Nicky's constant babbling. The music only adds to the chaos, so I quickly turn it off again. I'd like some ear plugs about now, or just some silence. Parents of nonverbal children have told me to be grateful that my child speaks. I am grateful, but sometimes it gets incredibly tedious to hear the same words over and over and over. Sometimes it is verbal torture.

Finally we arrive home. I turn off the engine with relief. One more time I hear Nicky quote *Farmyard Friends*: "In the summer, the sheep are sheared. They have their woolly coats cut off because they are too hot for them."

I am ready to bale out of the car but Mother grabs my wrist and squeezes it. "Wait," she whispers. She turns to Nicky and asks cautiously, "Nicky, are you feeling hot, like a sheep?"

His eyes lock to hers—a rare moment of eye contact. An unmistakable look of relief floods his face. "Yes," he says haltingly, "Nicky's too hot."
"Well let me get you out of here," she says. "I am so glad you could tell us how you were feeling!" She unbuckles his car seat and fans him with her crossword puzzle.

It's the middle of summer, but I feel a chill run up my spine. All this time in the hot car he has been trying to communicate! Only I wasn't listening. He is cutting and pasting words and phrases into his life, giving them new meaning. It simply sounded like rote memorization to me. How long has he been using these sound bites as a communication tool?

Inside the house Nicky goes directly to the tape player in his room. "Old MacDonald had a farm, E I E I O. . . ." But now, the familiar words and voice of the narrator haunt me: "In the summer, the sheep are sheared. They have their wooly coats cut off because they are too hot for them. . . ." I am the one who feels sheepish.

My therapist's office is in a small brick house with shutters. It is this English cottage look that probably keeps me wanting to come back. It seems so distant from my everyday reality. Here I can sit on a couch without juice stains, not step on spilled Cheerios. In this quiet room I can hear my own thoughts.

Even more important than place is my therapist, Gretchen, who listens. Listens. Listens. I am not afraid of being judged here. She does not try to tell me who I am or what to feel or how to be. I am finding that validation is one of the greatest gifts one human being can give another.

Through my tears I recount my feelings of helplessness—my fear of losing control when Nicky flies into a tantrum. When his tantrums first began, I was patient. But living with them day after day, my patience turned to anger. I find it hard to forgive myself for the times I have yelled at him in frustration or spanked him into compliance, especially those times before I knew about his autism. I have a hard time accepting my feelings, which still surface even though now I am aware of his disability.

"Anger is often an emotion that covers fear," Gretchen tells me gently. "If you step back and look deeper, is there fear hidden behind the anger?"

This concept startles me. I thought I was just an angry sort, a person with a short fuse. Me? Afraid?

"How do you feel when he explodes?" she asks.

"I want to make him stop. Isn't that my job, to calm him? I want to do the right thing. Fix him."

"But you can't, can you?"

Memories. I am a small child. My father is drunk and causing a scene. Who is this raging man? He was so nice to me this morning. Who is he now? What have I done? It must be my fault. My mother is crying, my brother has become invisible, my sister is hiding . . . I feel scared.

"You want things to stay calm and under control." Gretchen's voice gently brings me back. Her shutters filter the bright sunlight. The box of tissues waits for me on the table.

I suddenly see a parallel: when my son spins out of control, I am thrust back into my earliest fears about my own survival within a shattered family. My present feelings of helplessness are perhaps triggered by the Jekyll and Hyde aspect of Nicky that reminds me so much of life with my alcoholic parent.

I realize that I am safe with my child. I see that, in fact, I am an adult and have options that a five-year-old girl does not have. I am no longer powerless. I have choices. I can step back and breathe and realize that, even though I cannot control my son's rages, I can understand my feelings and react consciously. I can accept the fact that he does not have self-control yet, but I can imagine that someday he might.

For the first time, I forgive myself for not being "perfect." An unfamiliar warmth spreads throughout my body. Yes, awareness may be slow in coming, but I see that it can come. Gretchen hands me a card on which she has written the time of my next appointment.

The road is black and slick this afternoon. The air is filled with a fine drizzle. We are on a "car ride," one of Nicky's favorite activities since he was a baby. The boys and I talk about Halloween costumes and going to the pumpkin patch.

Steering around a curve, to my right, I see ferns and rocks clinging to the side of the hill. I do not see the three deer that dart out across the road. When I do, my foot slams on the brake and the car skids sideways, but there is a thump of an animal's hoof on the edge of the car's bumper.

A young fawn struggles up and hops into the forest. Upset and shaken, we get out of the car and peer into the woods. "Will Bambi be all right?" Ben asks tearfully. We watch the woods anxiously for several minutes, but there is no movement in the undergrowth. "I hope so, Honey," is all I can choke out.

Despite our desire, we are powerless to help this innocent creature. We reluctantly get back in the car. How quickly everything changes—one moment driving serenely along, the next jarred awake by the chance of death.

The next day a letter arrives, postmarked Texas. A letter from Sophie! Memories of college . . . playing Frisbee in the park, drinking cold beer after we closed the restaurant where we both worked. We used to spend hours talking about guys and trying to meet them. I remember when she met the man she would eventually marry, and how they roared away together on his motorcycle into the sunset.

I can't remember when I had last heard from her. I open the letter eagerly, drunk with memories of life when it was wilder, freer.

She writes, "We will be in the Northwest in a few weeks and would like to visit. I'm sorry I haven't written you sooner. We lost Megan, our little girl, to leukemia. She was so brave. . . ."

I fold the letter neatly, tucking it back into its envelope. I stare at it on the table. I turn it on each corner, over and over. Half in shock, I drift into the children's room, where four-year-old Ben naps in his bed. Breaking the unwritten mother's rule—never disturb a sleeping child—I gather him in my arms, breathe in the scent of his hair, and press his cheek to mine. I remember the fawn, imagine Sophie's little girl. My stomach contracts in deep, silent sobs. Ben's eyes flutter open, then close peacefully again as I rock him back to sleep.

Nicky at Six and a Half
An April rain has soaked the road. Today we have managed to break free of our boring Sunday chores and are driving up the river to the hot springs pool.

Rand and I talk a little about the houses along the river, and I dream aloud of having a cabin. "Wouldn't it be great to have a hideaway in the woods?" The groves of hazelnut trees, row after row of uniform intention, are beginning to blossom. My attention drifts from the fast moving scenes along the road: I am hypnotized by the yellow stripe rushing toward me. I snap back when an impatient voice behind me asks how much longer until we get to the hot pool.

We drive by a pasture full of cows. Nicky loves cows and now can name many.

"I see Jersey cows."

"Wow, there sure are a lot of them," I say. I know exactly what is coming next.

"Black cows are Angus cows. Guernseys are milk cows. White cows are Charlais."

"That's right, Nicky. You really like cows, don't you?" I try to extend the possibilities for communicating beyond mere identification.

Ben is absorbed in a book. I turn to Rand, who is tuned out. I look back at the road, which rushes toward me through a green tunnel of fir trees. I wish I were a hawk soaring over the valley.

A very small, uncertain voice brings me back to the car. I do not know this voice, but it comes from Nicky. I am afraid to turn around, afraid I will interrupt this rarity. I tap Rand on the arm and motion for him to listen.

Nicky sings, "I love this car ride. This is so good. All the trees, and the cows, and the mountains. I feel so good and happy."

His own words! His own happy thoughts! Words that don't come from a video or a book or a song. Words that spring from within him! This song rushes over me and fills me with hope.

The singing lasts about a minute. I've held my breath through most of it, and through eyes brimming with joyful tears, I turn to Nicky. "Will you sing some more? I love your song!"

He looks out the window and says, "My favorite cows are Guernseys; they are milk cows."

I sit in a playroom crowded with physical therapists. It is filled with swings, toys, small stairs to climb, and other enticements to help young bodies and minds become more flexible, more able. Everyone here has the best of intentions. They have chosen this field, most of them, because they want to help others. I am attending an assembly at which a renowned therapist will demonstrate a particular technique on two children with autism.

My son is first. I feel tentative but happy that he

was asked to be a guinea pig. On one hand, I'm sure that he will not cooperate. On the other, I am excited that he will receive a free therapy session with such a highly regarded professional.

Nicky doesn't surprise me. He is uncooperative, as expected. He is understandably confused that this usually private playroom is full of adults sitting in a half-circle and taking up too much space. Where is his regular therapist? She is there, but she explains to him that someone else will be working with him for just a little while. I have offered the reward of ice cream to follow, and I remind him of this at least twenty times to motivate him to participate.

He sits alone on the floor lining up colored blocks. The therapist approaches and begins her rather invasive technique of muscular release. He yells at her, "Leave me alone!" She persists. Quite a scene ensues. All I can think about is how I've taught my son to use his words so that others will understand his needs—now he is clearly telling her to get away and she is ignoring him for the sake of the demonstration.

Eventually, my son fights his way out of there. He screams, he bites, he runs. I feel I have betrayed him in a way, because I did not thoroughly think through how much the technique might bother him or how upsetting this would be for him. He has gone into a familiar room in the back and agrees to play while I watch what happens with the next child.

The little girl is brought in through the front door. Her mother has timed their arrival perfectly, as often children with autism have a hard time relaxing in any environment, let alone in a small room full of strange people. She is less verbal than my son, but she is able say a few halting words.

"Fwower, fwower," she repeats several times, pointing to the window. It is spring. Plum trees shower pink flowers in the wet wind. "Fwower," again. Even garbled it is obvious that she is excited by the show of petals.

"Flower is her new word. That is all she thinks about," says her mother, in that familiar, almost apologetic voice which intones so much. (I'm sorry my child is perseverating, I'm sorry my child repeats. . . .)

All the therapists look out the window once and agree that the flowers are pretty. But there is a conference to run, and the first child was so uncooperative. Let's get this show on the road, is the unmistakable feeling in the room.

The therapist hands her a toy. The toy is flung aside.

"Fwower!" A small finger points to the trees outside the window.

"Yes, sweetie, there are flowers outside, but we are going to play with some toys," says the therapist.

"Fwower!"

Now at least two more well-intentioned students attempt to engage her with something in the room. Someone hands her a doll.

The little girl points to the doll and lets out an enthusiastic, "Fwower!" She looks excited.

"No, sweetie, that is not a flower, that is a doll. D-O-L-L, a dolly you can play with," says the professional, speaking slowly and clearly, with the authority of a teacher. She begins the muscular release technique on the unsuspecting child.

"Fwower, fwower, fwower." The little girl points at the doll, her voice escalating.

"Doll, doll, doll," repeats the therapist.

Finally, the child flings the doll across the room and runs to a swinging chair, the therapists following her. The doll lands near my feet. I pick it up to put it away. I look at the small print on the dress and swallow hard. From a distance the print had looked like dots, but on closer look I see that it is a pattern of flowers. I go and get Nicky from the other room. We leave through the back door and step out onto a sidewalk of plum petals.

Chapter 4

What is life? It is the flash of a firefly in the night. It is the breath of a buffalo in the winter-time. It is the little shadow which runs across the grass and loses itself in the sunset. (Crowfoot)

Nicky at Seven

Every time I give Nicky a kiss he wipes it away with his hand as if it were repulsive. I know it isn't me; I know it is a "sensory issue" or a "compulsive act," more features of autism. Understanding doesn't make this small act hurt any less.

One day I blurt out, "Please don't wipe my kiss away, rub it in and make it stay." Something about the rhyme makes him laugh. Something in him is freed up. Perhaps he understands the importance the kiss carries for both of us. Perhaps he wants to oblige me in this small happiness?

"Kiss me again," he insists. The hand brushes up to the cheek in the usual fashion, but this time he smiles and says, "I rub it in to make it stay. Kiss me again."

I kiss his cheek, his forehead, the top of his head, over and over. Each time his hand goes up and grinds the kiss in. Laughing, and trying to look into his eyes if only for a brief second, I say, "Thank you, Nicky, for letting me show you my love with a kiss."   Very tenderly, he bends over and kisses my cheek. My hand reaches upward, covering this invisible gift, rubbing it in, making it stay.

It is Jill's last day as a volunteer in our home program. I've watched her evolve from a timid girl into a confident teacher to my son. Today, her long blond hair is up in a bun, and her blue eyes twinkle as she and Nicky share a snack of crackers and juice.

"What will you choose to play with after snack, Nicky?" she asks brightly.

"Lincoln Logs," comes a reply that doesn't surprise me. I've noticed that he likes to play certain games with particular people, and Lincoln Log house building is his favorite with Jill.

For the longest time he wouldn't let her touch the houses he built. Eventually, she was able to build a shed near him. Today, they build the log house together.

Jill, like Nicky, also has a favorite activity. She has tried for months, without success, to teach Nicky the song, "Little Cabin in the Woods." Never once has he honored her request to sing along.

When they have finished building the log house, Nicky wants to act out "The Three Little Pigs." He is the big bad wolf and delights in growling at Jill. Despite the fact that this looks like imaginary play, it is still extremely routine, with Nicky insisting on sameness each time. The dialogue must be verbatim from the Disney story tape he has. However, Jill tries to interject new elements, and over the months he has learned to tolerate this. Today Practical Pig tells the wolf he should brush his teeth.

The hour passes quickly. "Nicky," Jill says quietly, "I have something to tell you. Can you look at me?" Nicky, back at the log house, glances up and then back down as he readjusts the chimney.

"This is the last day I will come play with you.

I love you and I will miss you very much," she continues.

Nicky does not say a word or show any emotion. Although she hides it, I know Jill wishes he could acknowledge what she says. She tells him it is time to clean up the playroom and gets up to brush off the table.

Nicky doesn't move, but crashes the log house. "Oh Nicky," says Jill, not surprised, "now you'll have to clean that up too."

He starts to build it up again, only this time he sings something softly under his breath. I lean closer to the monitor so I can hear what it is, but one look on Jill's face tells me.

A small voice, with perfect pitch, floats across the room: "Little cabin in the woods, little man by the window stood, saw a rabbit hopping by, knocking at his door. . . ."

We drive around in circles, looking for space B-24. Men in plaid shorts are lighting fires in pits. Women up to their ears in plastic food storage containers are yelling at kids who are chasing dogs and knocking over lawn chairs.

Rand and I have separated. I am nervous because it is the first time I've taken the kids camping without him. Some of my friends have invited me to join them on their annual Fourth of July camp-out. Sarah, Chris, Anna, Josh, George, and about seven other people have all assembled here at the coast.

After winding around and around, I finally spot Mike's big gold and white tent. We tumble out of the car. Nicky hates this unfamiliar campground. Everything feels wrong to him. He usually likes to camp and generally likes the beach. Why didn't it occur to me that a new place with new people might upset him this much? It did occur to me. New experiences with Nicky are like playing the lottery. The odds of winning are not in my favor.

Before I have a chance to begin unpacking, Nicky and Ben dash off down the trail to the ocean. I can't let them go alone. Nicky shows no understanding of sneaker waves, drowning, or any dangers associated with the rough Oregon coast.

This beach is not to his liking. There are too many rocks and not enough sand. He hates the crows that caw eerily and swoop down to pick garbage off the beach. Worse yet, children are setting off rounds of firecrackers.

"Too much loudness, too much loudness!" he says again and again.

Finally, I bury him in the sand. The heat and the pressure relax him. As long as I am there with him, pouring more sand on top of him, he stays calm. Only a small moon of his face is uncovered.

Josh and Anna who have been sitting a distance away, watching, wander over with their daughter Rose. "All I can say is, this is some heavy karma," says Josh. I bite my lip and continue to heap sand on top of my child. Josh offers to pitch our tent.

I smile at him gratefully. "Do you owe me a favor from a past life?" Joking helps relieve my tension.

Nicky and I spend the next two hours in the tent trying to keep occupied and comfortable. He wants to go home.

"Home is a long way away," I tell him. This just makes him more anxious. Ben and his friend, Sam, run around and find things to do—they play ball, they play Frisbee. Nicky cannot find the fun in any of the things they do. I read thirteen books to him until he falls into a nap.

In the evening, at the fire circle, he is content to light a long stick and carefully blow it out, or extinguish it in a bucket of water sitting next to him. He does this quietly over and over. This is something we let him do when it is just our family camping. For a few precious moments I relax. Another parent, whom I have only been introduced to, decides that if one child is allowed to do this all the others kids will want to do it too. Naturally, this won't do; it would be too dangerous; someone will get burned. . . . Even though I'm sitting right there with him, she pressures me to make him stop doing the one activity that he enjoys doing independently.

I understand her concern. When I tell him it is time to stop, he erupts in a fit of rage. I drag him to the car. I am hoping it will muffle his screaming. It is one thing to deal with his outbursts in the privacy of our home, but a tent in a crowded campground offers no buffer. I consider packing everything up and driving home, but I don't want to let him "win."

Later that night, after the boys are asleep, George, a man I have met but do not know well, comes up to me and says, "I don't know how you do it. I thought parenting was hard, but I had no idea. . . ." I know he is trying to be kind, but what I don't want or need is pity. I nod, smile at him faintly, and walk alone into the night.

The next morning Nicky and I walk around and around and around the campground. It is something to do. His map-like mind has already memorized the many cul-de-sacs of the campground. Campers stare at us as if we are nuts.   Twenty-five times around and I begin to learn the names of their dogs.

We discover that there are hot showers! How could we have missed this yesterday? It is like finding an oasis in the desert. I sit in front of the concrete building reading a book for an hour while Nicky sits in the steaming shower room, singing. It is a good thing there is more than one shower. I do not look up at the campers standing in line for a turn.

The day wears on. At three o'clock, Nicky finishes his fourth shower. Sarah insists that I take a break and drive over to see the botanical gardens a few miles south. She assures me that with all the adults around they will be able to handle Nicky for an hour or two. She offers me respite. At this moment it feels like the kindest thing anyone has ever done for me.

In the rearview mirror, I see my son run down the road chasing my car, screaming for me to stop. Should I slam on the brakes and turn around? Sarah sprints after him and Mike heads him off at the pass.

I look again and see Nicky's blond head bobbing upside down as Mike carries him back to our camp like a sack of potatoes. Turning onto the highway, I gulp in breaths of warm salt air—hungry for this taste of freedom.

"Fred, I am looking for the song that goes, 'Da da Dum, da da Dum, da da Dum Dum Dum.'" I hum the tune to my friend who works at the record store.

"Oh, that's, um, that's . . . the 'William Tell Over-ture' . . . hmm, Rossini." He retrieves a cassette tape from the classical section.

"Nicky loves this song," I tell him. "He heard it in an old cartoon and loves to conduct it like Mickey Mouse."

"I don't know many seven-year-olds with musical taste beyond Alvin and the Chipmunks," Fred says appreciatively.

I hide this surprise in my purse. I am tempted to leave it there. So many times I have tried to engage Nicky in a game or new activity only to have him roll away on the floor uninterested. I've introduced toys that I thought would delight him, only to watch him fling them across the room.

"What if," I think, doubtfully, "this isn't the correct arrangement of the 'William Tell Overture'?"

Nevertheless, later that afternoon, when we are alone, I tell him I have a surprise. I pull the tape out of my purse. Immediately, he jumps up and runs out of the room covering his ears. "Not a new song, not a new song," he yells.

Fumbling with the tape-player, I wonder why I bother. Is it worth the battle to try to bring anything new into his life? There are times when I want to give up. But then, where would that leave me? Where would that leave him? I push "play." The music begins quietly, then builds to the recognizable sounds of the song.

Nicky appears from behind a corner. His eyes are open wide. "It's 'William Tell'," he squeals and rushes toward me. He hugs my legs and then sits directly in front of the stereo speaker, ear pressed against it. A feeling of unbounded joy overtakes me as we unite in this measure of sound.

Nicky cannot keep his eyes from wandering. He looks at the cabin and the barn as he "drives," sitting on my lap, hands on the wheel, up the long gravel road to Jane's house. Her thirty-seven-year-old horse, Cyrus, and her burro, Don Quixote, graze in the front meadow. Sometimes, we might spy in the oak grove a family of deer, frozen and watchful until our car passes.

Jane meets us at the door, her arms wide open. She gives strong and vigorous hugs. The boys do not linger, though. They are off looking for Kitty White Face and Kitty Black, who have no doubt run for cover at the sound of four small boot-clad feet.

They run to the familiar pleasures . . . wooden statues of birds, streamers, art supplies, and piles of quilts to hide under in an upstairs closet. Jane is like a grandmother to them.

Nicky has his routines, his rituals that apply when he is at Jane's house. When we eat our snack, he asks for the tiny blue glass that he loves and a small silver pitcher filled with apple cider.

"Cheers," he says, beaming, holding the little blue glass high. Because it is only good for one gulp he fills it again and again. We toast to everyone and everything we can think of.

He then usually starts to talk about videos, and after listening a minute, we politely ask him to be quiet. Ben and Jane use this time to catch up on things, while Nicky busies himself with the up and down lever of the office chair he prefers to sit on.

When the food is eaten, we set off on a predictable path—first across a log spanning a gully, then down to the pond, where the boys will scoop out duckweed and look for frogs. Sometimes the boys throw rocks in the pond, and this usually gets way out of hand, with Jane asking them please not to deplete her entire driveway.

From there, Nicky leads the way to the small cabin that was built by one of the first pioneers in this town. Jane's art studio is here. The boys try on a large snake mask and spend a few moments drawing pictures.

Off to the oak tree. Huge and old, it waits patiently. The boys climb high into it and look over the valley. In its limbs they actually grow quiet for a time, and they are usually in no hurry to climb down.

Sooner or later they decide it is time to feed the animals. Cyrus and Don Quixote get grains and carrots. The boys stroke the horse's nose, but Donqui is too shy to be petted and eats his food away from the barn.

Sometimes Nicky and Ben take a bath in an old iron claw-foot tub that sits hidden behind the woodshed, just on the edge of the woods. Unlike home, here the children can splash water everywhere and I don't have to yell at them about making a mess. That is the beauty of being here with Jane. She understands Nicky's needs and ways; there is no need to explain anything.

Often I sit in a comfortable chair sipping tea, or I take a nap in the hammock, while Jane plays with the boys. Jane actually insists on this, and I would be a fool to argue with her. At times I sit a distance away from them, on an island between two creeks. The water, the sounds, flow around me. I feel the present already becoming a future memory. My body stores in its cells this time of peace.

Chapter 5

In the first grade my teacher took me outside. She handed me a prism and a white piece of paper. She gave me a tool that could unlock sunlight. I hung around school eleven more years, waiting for another moment like that.

Nicky at Seven and a Half

I stand in front of the bright green door, waiting to pick Nicky up from class. As we walk to our car I spot another small boy ahead of us. "Look," I say to Nicky, "that boy is wearing a sweater like yours!" I am trying to engage Nicky's interest—he likes sharks, which are the theme of the sweaters. It does interest him, and he looks down at his sweater and says, directly quoting from *Reptiles of the Amazon*, "You know, Mom, sharks do not have bones, only cartilage."

"Very good," I say, "but what is that boy's name?" I am curious to know if my child is learning the names of his classmates after three months of school. One of our goals for him is to become more socially aware.

"I don't know," he replies.

We get in the car. "Come on," I badger, "you know his name, I know you do, tell me what it is."

"I don't know."

"Think, Nicky, come on, you can do it." For some reason, I'm determined that he try. This pushing goes on for at least two minutes. I see his small hand grip the door handle tightly. His eyes close, and with the greatest effort and concentration he begins:

"Good afternoon, class. Good afternoon, Haley, good afternoon, John, good afternoon, Brittany, good afternoon, Cory, good afternoon, Aleisha, good afternoon, Mark, good afternoon Ray, good afternoon Garrett. That's it, good afternoon, Garrett."

Stunned, I thank him for telling me his classmate's name (which I assume is just Garrett and not Good Afternoon Garrett). For the first time I understand the way his brain works differently from mine. I truly "get" it. His is a brain of cul de sacs and one-way streets. There are no shortcuts. As I drive home

I wonder what it would be like to be able to travel only down one-way streets. It would take us hours to get home, and it would be a miracle if we arrived at all.

Kim looks like any other first-grader, with her long brown hair and plaid skirt. Her mother, Eileen, points her out to me across the loud, crowded lunchroom. Kids file past me, dumping chocolate milk containers into a big gray garbage can, and stare at me because I'm an unfamiliar face. We walk over and sit at the table next to Kim.

"Kim, this is Elizabeth. She is here to look at your artwork. Can you say 'Hi'?"

"Hi." Kim speaks to the wall in front of her and takes one last bite of her peanut butter and jelly sandwich. She watches me from the corner of her eye. I tell Kim that I really like her drawings and that I'm going to produce greeting cards from some of them.

"Would that be OK with you?" I ask. She looks directly at me and nods. I feel as though she has given me a diamond.

Eileen and I walk to their small, cozy house not far from the school. She tells me about Kim, about how they had difficulty from the start, even before they discovered that she had autism. As a baby, Kim cried continuously night and day. Eileen suffered from severe sleep deprivation. When she got older, Kim became what is known as a "bolter," that is, she would slip out of the house whenever she got the chance. Eileen and her husband, John, eventually had to secure their house with key bolts and an alarm system because Kim quickly figured out how to open any locks.

At four, Kim could speak very few words. Eileen saw Kim draw a circle, a triangle—an ice cream cone! Eileen asked her if she would like one. "Yes!" After that, a new form of communication emerged for Kim. Eileen and John encouraged her to draw more.

Kim began attending kindergarten at a regular school when she was six. Although the teacher and assistants had received a little training about autism, they had had no hands-on experience. Kim's vocabulary was still quite limited, and the words she could speak always seemed out of context. After being in school two weeks, the teachers could see no indications that the lessons they taught were reaching her at all.

During this period of transition into school, Kim coped with the change and stimulation by drawing about fifty pages a day. Sometimes she would draw the same thing maybe fifteen times.

"We were wading in paper," Eileen tells me. "One evening, while trying to control the flow of paper in the living room, I heard Kim say, 'One, two . . . four . . . six, seven.' I corrected her over and over, telling her how to count. After she had gone to bed that night, John and I looked over some of her drawings. We found one particularly interesting . . . it showed a shoe, a chicken, some three dimensional planks, and a door. Usually, the subjects in Kim's drawings relate to each other, but we couldn't figure this one out.

"The next morning, John called Kim over to him to name the objects on the paper. He came to the conclusion that it might possibly represent the nursery rhyme, 'One, Two, Buckle my Shoe.'

"Later that day, we showed it to the teacher. She gazed at it in amazement. All week they had practiced counting by repeating the rhyme. But the teacher hadn't been sure if Kim was understanding or even listening to the lesson. Now the teacher knew that what she was teaching did reach Kim, that it was getting through to her." Eileen tells me that after that, everyone at the school treated Kim with greater respect.

It takes me quite a while to look at all of Kim's drawings. They are exquisite, beautiful expressions. There is the drawing of a conductor and a complete orchestra of instruments—without musicians. I hold up the one of a girl, a boy, and a nurse bringing flowers to a sick patient. I wonder where her inspirations come from.

As if reading my mind, Eileen picks up a drawing whose delicate lines reveal feeling and sentiment at first glance. "You might find it interesting that Kim starts with a detail like this bow on the dress and draws outward."

"Incredible," I say. "So she must know exactly what she wants to draw and how it will look when she starts."

"Maybe," says Eileen. "With Kim it's hard to know, hard to tell." She runs her fingers over the drawing of a child holding the hand of a woman who is walking with an umbrella. "This one is my favorite. She drew it before she could hold my hand. Like a lot of kids with autism, she found it painful and would wince when I held hers. I think that it was her way of telling me that she would do it if she were able to."

Nodding, I carefully place this drawing in the pile that will go home with me. Each one of them "speaks" a thousand words.

A Month From My Journal

January first. It's a brave New Year. I eat black-eyed peas and open the package of narcissus bulbs I received as a Christmas gift. Two more days until school starts again. It's been a nice break for the kids to be away from the pressures of school, but like all good moms, I'm ready for vacation to end. The lunch boxes are waiting like soldiers on the top of the fridge. I guess we need to get ready for "transition issues." With autism, it's always "transition issues."

I'm glad Nicky is succeeding in a regular education class. He couldn't do it, though, without the full-time aide. It's only January. Do I need to start preparing my data sheets and requests to make sure Nicky gets all the help he needs? How hard will I have to push this year for services?

January third. It is rough getting Nicky back in school. I wonder how many times he will bolt in the next few weeks. If my senses were screwed up like his, I'd want to run too. It's funny how sometimes he will say, "That violin sound *looks* beautiful," or "I *see* the sound of that bell."

January seventh. I've been asked by the School District to attend a one-day brainstorming session concerning services for children with disabilities. I am supposed to recruit more parents. Why is it that most of the parents I talk to would rather be mopping their floors?

January fifteenth. Two fellow mothers of children with disabilities and I head up to Portland today to see a friend. Our child-care arrangements altogether probably took ten hours of planning. Stopping first at the bakery to load up on cinnamon rolls, orange twists, and coffee, we eventually accelerate north. Twenty minutes of nervous chitchat ensues before we start talking about why we're making this trip.

Our friend Amy's little boy, Justin, has been in the Intensive Care Unit at a hospital in Portland for over six weeks. We thought he'd be home for Christmas. Justin has Down Syndrome. He's had open- heart surgery and a pacemaker operation and has multiple infections. He's on a respirator, but he's hanging on.

Amy had been worried about Justin for weeks, but the doctors kept telling her that he would be OK. They failed to administer a simple blood test for anemia. Justin's condition worsened until an emergency blood tranfusion was required. During this surgery Justin "coded." They had to airlift him to Portland. I learned that "coded" means that he clinically died for a brief moment. Sometimes I hate the vocabulary of our lives.

When we arrive at the hospital, Amy and her husband meet us at the door of the ICU. She is beyond exhaustion—her face a paler shade of white than the hospital sheets. We don yellow robes, gloves, and masks and enter Justin's room. There are so many tubes and machines, and he's so little. My eyes well up. He wakes up and smiles at his Daddy. Something in my heart lets go. His arms may be strapped down, but those little legs are moving with all he's got.

We get Amy out of there for lunch. She lets it out. We all cry. We manage to laugh, too. After lunch, we head home, still digesting it all. That night I see that the narcissus bulbs are sprouting.

January twentieth. Everyone in this family has the flu. In and out of school. I don't think I'll be able to have a "real" job for a while yet. Maybe I could keep my mail-order book business going until Nicky graduates and then employ him. I never thought I'd be planning life twelve years in advance.

January twenty-fifth. The insurance company is giving us the run around again about occupational therapy services for Nicky. I guess with the new year they figure it's prime time to try to withhold coverage once again. I write my fourth letter to the approval committee. Will this never end? Ben asks me if he can catch autism. I love volunteering in Ben's class. Feeling like just another mom for an hour a week is refreshing.

January twenty-seventh. I attend the School District seminar. It goes surprisingly well. People meet people and put faces to names. Community is important; it's all we've got. It is weird, though, to be dreaming about ideal services when we know twelve million dollars of the school's budget will be cut. I hear most people saying that a wide range of services is imperative. Also, if inclusion is to work, training and support must be provided for teachers, whose load is already too heavy. I hear a parent say she is "terrified" of inclusion. We want choices. We want what our children are legally entitled to. We want the best for all children.

January thirty-first. Ah . . . the Sunday paper . . . City Region section: proposed cuts in the School District identified by the superintendent include "eliminating" special education teachers, "eliminating" school bus service, "eliminating" sixteen instructional assistants, among many other things. So much for idealism. I feel sick. I crawl back into bed. Later, after mopping the floor, I discover that the narcissus are blooming.

Nicky at Eight

In the playground, swings are pendulums against the sky and children team like ants on a wooden play structure. Some are playing ball in the field. It is loud even from here, near the school walls and well away from the commotion. It does not take me long to spot my child. He is the one on the edge of everything, wandering around looking at flowers and talking to himself. A tight knit ski cap identifies him too. It is more than out of place considering that it is a warm April day. He looks like a Smurf, one of those lovable cartoon characters that live in their own world.

"Elizabeth, you've got to get him out of that hat." The voice of his aide almosts arrests me with its shrillness.

"It makes him stand out and look so weird."

She's right, of course, it does. Beyond that, I've learned that the feeling of the hat gives him comfort and sensory input. He obviously doesn't care that he looks weird; why should I? Because everybody else can't seem to stand it? Because it is my "job" to make him fit in as much as possible?

I will wrestle with this issue our whole life, I think. Right now, I want him to be happy and comfortable and to make it through school one more day. That's all. Maybe the hat will come off before the Fourth of July, and maybe it won't.

I am dressed in a dark blue suit and I look as though I should be attending either a power lunch on Wall Street or a funeral. I am about to attend an Individualized Education Plan (IEP) meeting for Nicky at his

74

school, and power dressing is just another trick I've learned over the last couple of years. I'm ready to play hard ball; I'm acting the part.

I have brought a friend with me, to take notes, to hear what I cannot hear because of the emotions I know will get in the way. It promises to be a rough meeting.

Seven school district personnel are already assembled when we enter the room.

"Does anyone mind if I tape the meeting?" I ask politely, placing a small black recorder in the middle of the table. The atmosphere is chilly on this bright June afternoon.

"Who is this person? Why is she here?" asks one of the staff.

"She is my advocate," I say, drawing a deep breath. "I've asked her to come and listen and take notes." Smile.

What they are not acknowledging is that it is intimidating for a parent to sit at a table full of professionals who speak jargon, who all get paid from the same pot, who all eat lunch together, and who assess and judge your child in the teacher's lounge.

The year has not been easy, with Nicky still having difficulty understanding and performing everything that is expected of him. Even with the support of a one-on-one assistant, he is struggling. It is a complicated mess, which needs to be sorted out piece by piece.

They want him gone; he's too much trouble. I know that, even though nobody has said it. It is easier to shuffle children around sometimes than to take the necessary steps to make the situation work. This goes on all the time. Students are regrouped and sent to new "centers" almost yearly. I know of one child who has attended four different schools in five years.

I feel that Nicky needs to stay where he is. This will mark the end of three years of inclusion in a regular education classroom, and he has made improvements. Moreover, he is familiar and comfortable with the school, and the children in his class understand him. I see it as imperative that he stay.

I shift uncomfortably on the pint-sized child's schoolroom chair on which I sit. I have sat through many of these meetings quietly, nodding, trying to be a "good parent." Trying to "get along," not "make waves." Looking back, I realize that these meetings make me feel as though I'm in grade school again and have been called to the office for doing something naughty. Why else would I be meeting with the school principal?

I wonder how often the administration banks on this subconscious fear and feeling of inadequacy, and on the lack of power the typical parent like me must feel. We are so very out of place. Neither a student nor a teacher. Our children are viewed as "problems." How often do they size parents up—this one's got some education . . . this family has some money . . . this family won't know any better—and then offer the minimum amount of services? After all, budgets can only stretch so far.

The tester removes his glasses and runs his fingers over his eyes as though he has a headache. He has tested my son's cognitive skills. He has administered the test without consulting us as to what might have been used (stickers, M&Ms . . .) to motivate Nicky to answer the questions. We wanted Nicky's scores to reflect his actual cognitive abilities, not his ability to "test."

"The results," he informs me, shaking his head, "would indicate that your son is a nonreader." He drones on for another twenty minutes, finishing with the pronouncement, "Your son's placement at this school has been a failure."

Shock and rage boil inside me like lava. I erupt.

"My son has learned how to walk in a line, he has learned how to raise his hand, he has learned how to sit in class, he no longer runs away, he has participated in school performances. How dare you call my son's time here a failure!" I hardly believe my own voice. I am shaking. The insensitivity of this man is the last straw. Having just completed a special-education law class this term, I quote the "stay put" provision, which guarantees a parent's right to appeal any decision regarding a change in their child's placement.

The atmosphere in the room changes. The teacher is in tears. The principal assures me that it can be worked out. This seems like a bad dream. I gather my recorder, my notebook, and my dignity and exit stage right.

Chapter 6

"People think angels fly because they have wings. Angels fly because they take themselves lightly."

(G. K. Chesterton)

Nicky at Nine

A woman's magazine seduces me into believing that I can share a joyful day with my children creating a gingerbread house. I cut out a picture of the most beautiful one, tape it to my refrigerator, and imagine basking in glowing satisfaction, like the two-dimensional family in front of me. I honestly forget that this picture is just a prop.

I recall that my sister, having lived in Munich during her junior year in high school, became an amateur/professional gingerbread-house maker. One of her creations once sold for twenty-five dollars while on display in the lobby of her apartment building in

New York City. Considering her an expert, I phone her immediately.

"They're tricky," she warns. "Are you sure you want to get into this?" I insist. She advises me how to cut out a cardboard pattern and how to whip up a stiff frosting. I furiously jot down notes.

Math has never been my forte. Attempts to enlarge the three-inch patterns from the *Ladies Home Journal* yields piece after piece of grid-paper transformed to wadded balls of frustration. The boys enjoy a good indoor snowball fight with them.

We head for the store to buy all the supplies. One hundred dollars later I leave the discount food warehouse with enough bridge mix to see my grandmother's card group through a year of Thursdays. We arrive home, but I realize I've forgotten the molasses.

I strap the kids back in the car and head for a convenience store, fully ready to shell out ten dollars for a jar of molasses if it means I can leave the kids in the car. But molasses is too obscure for the 7 Eleven, so it's another trip to the grocery store.

Nicky insists on choosing a coupon from each of the blinking dispensers on each of the fourteen aisles. Meanwhile, Ben scores as many free samples as possible from the ladies demonstrating the latest microwave food-type substance. I buy two jars of molasses, just in case. Glancing at the magazines next to the cashier, I notice that three out of five feature gingerbread houses. I curse them under my breath.

"Who is going to help me make the dough?" I ask when we get home. Nicky tries, but finds he hates the smell of molasses and runs screaming out of the kitchen. Ben stays to help.

Carefully cutting the pieces from rolled gingerbread dough, I think things might work out. Then the phone rings; it is my friend, Janice. I invite her over to help decorate the gingerbread house. In my absence Ben eats half of the raw dough. I am short the roof, and must make another batch. I send Ben to his room for an extended time out. I find myself alone with this *family* project.

The baked pieces break when I try to remove them from the pan. Refusing to give up, I make another batch. By seven PM, I have enough whole gingerbread pieces to make a modest, no frills tract house.

Janice, who has no children but works with them as a physical therapist, arrives to help me decorate

81

the gingerbread house. I push dough-plastered hair out of my face and try to think of something imaginative to do, but there is not a creative drop left in me. The children show very little interest in decorating; they just want to eat the candy. Meanwhile, Janice fashions miniature sleighs out of foil for the Gummi Bears, artfully placing them on the "snow-covered" roof. She has a great time cutting licorice windowpanes and making candy cane sidewalks. I put two sugar-hyped kids to bed and let her finish the entire thing.

When I wake up the next morning, I remember that there will be a beautiful gingerbread house gracing my table. Perhaps it was worth all the hassle. I pad into the dining room to see this beautiful product of such frustrating effort.

A brown blob has fallen on the rug. The carport has collapsed, and half the house has been eaten. My dog lies in the corner, a Gummi Bear sledding down a big hunk of frosting that has stuck onto her nose.

I'm dreaming of the shining faces of my children as they listen rapturously to classical music at a December children's concert. It is being held at the grand old music hall at the University, where velvet cords hold you back from the balcony, where the pipe organ rises into the high ceiling. Dreaming, and resisting reality, are coping mechanisms of mine.

With much protest, the kids and I, along with my friend Larry and his son, Joe, set off.

"Why do we have to go there?" my children wail.

"Because it is music. You both like music. It is Christmas, and it is something to do. Because I want to take you, and I want a Christmas memory!"

The resistance continues. By the time we get to the hall and settle in our seats I am exhausted. Then bad luck arrives. Several very tall people sit directly in front of us.

Ben jumps up, "I'm moving, I can't see." Joe follows.

This, of course, upsets Nicky, who had almost resigned himself to the whole thing, but this quick change is not to his liking and a conniption fit is about to begin. After some some quick cajoling, we move to new seats.

Now it is time to carefully dole out the first piece of candy. Larry is cracking up at my strategy. We all sit sucking on Tootsie Rolls. All is well for about two minutes.

Nicky begins to complain loudly, and heads turn ever so discreetly. I imagine what they are thinking and look down at my lovely black velvet shoes. Ben and Joe are wiggling on the top of their folded-up seats until—thump—they fall. My dirty looks are in vain. I can only hiss at them.

I am about to throw in the towel, but miraculously the concert begins. The boys actually listen to the first piece! I begin to loosen my iron grip on the chair arm.

As the conductor turns to explain the next piece, Nicky loudly asks, "Mom, why did you bring me here to listen to all these flutes, clarinets, bassoons, kettle drums, oboes, tubas, trumpets, piccolos, and xylophones?"

All heads turn, and I believe I hear a chuckle pass over the woodwinds. I sigh.

"For the memories, Honey, for the memories."

Here in the mountains the air is sharp and clear. I look out of the cabin onto the white expanse of snow, excited about the change of scenery. We are three adults and three kids in search of play. We've brought all the right ingredients for a good time: hot chocolate, sleds, and board games.

The boys make snowmen, get cold, and run back in to get warm before the fire. As I unpack the food, I hear John say loudly, "Ben, you retard!" I cringe. Nobody else seems to notice.

I used to say it as a kid and never thought anything of it. "You're a retard!" Anything uncool was retarded. But because of Nicky and the work I've started to do with disability issues, my awareness of this word as an insult cuts deep.

I remember when I was in grade school. I'd watch the kids with disabilities walk single-file into the lunch room just as we other kids were licking the last drops of chocolate milk from our lips. We would watch as they went to their own table, away from us, to eat. I still remember the little girl with a giant head and the boy in the wheelchair. The teachers never talked to us about them or integrated them into any of our activities. To us they were "the retarded kids." No one would have been caught dead talking to them. By the time they sat down to eat it was time for the rest of us to have recess. There was no "mainstreaming," no "inclusion," and no mention of the kids with disabilities.

"You're a retard, Ben!" John is stuck on that word. I've heard it three times in the last hour. Why am I remaining silent? It occurs to me that if he had said "nigger" or expressed some other racial slur I'd be all over his case. But terms that indicate fear and loathing of people with disabilities, terms like "moron," "cretin," "retard," and "lame," are used every day. They are socially acceptable to many.

They aren't acceptable to me anymore. Words have power. Words affect our attitudes. I call John aside and explain to him why I'd like him to stop using that word. He half rolls his eyes and shrugs. "Whatever," he says. But he stops.

An ironic synchronicity occurs later that evening during a scrabble game. I do a double take at the letters in front of me. There, in my little wooden tile holder, rest six letters and the possibility of a double word score. The letters are R-E-T-A-R-D. Placing the letters on the board, I emphatically define the meaning for the other players. "Re-*tard*" is a verb:

"to make slow or delay the progress of." I reiterate, "Re-*tard*" is a verb.

"I'm going to get you, and when I do, you won't have a chance. . . ."

"Why you little. . . ."

Nicky and his friend, Alito, roll around on the floor, wrestling. Squeals of laughter erupt from Nicky as he tries to squirm away and pin Alito to the floor. Suddenly, Ben runs into the room and jumps headlong into the heap. Arms and legs flailing, eyes wide and wild, they spin and tumble all over the living room. The three of them are more entertaining to watch than pro-wrestlers on television. I'm so pleased Nicky has a friend. Never mind that he is forty.

Nicky met Alito one evening at a dance in the park. As people sway and rock to the music I see my kids literally jumping on a small man with a wild mane of black curls. He flips the kids around and rolls away like an acrobat. Just as I'm about to go rescue this stranger, my friend, Debbie, stops me.

"That's Alito Alessi," she says. "He is a dancer who conducts workshops for people with disabilities. Relax, let them dance."

When the music is over, Nicky says, "I made a friend. He danced and wrestled with me." Nicky appears so happy. I realize how rare it is for him to be excited about being with a person. I look around for this new friend, but he is lost in the crowd. I decide to learn more about this man and what he does.

The next day I am on the phone with Alito. He tells me of his work, the DanceAbility Project. He teaches workshops all over the world, where people with varying degrees of physical ability come together to dance. "I am not a therapist," he states emphatically, "I'm a dancer." He gives me an example of the method of his work:

"Once in Austria they wheel a woman into the room on a bed. She is paralyzed, and she can't speak English. Anyway, I have to think fast. I realize she can move her eyes, and we can all move our eyes. I find the common denominator within the group and start from there. By the end of the class she is choreographing an entire dance with her eyes. We roll her bed around, we dance around her, she dances with us, we ALL dance. The work is about creating new realities, where people express themselves no matter what their abilities are."

I offer Alito money to come work with Nicky, but he refuses it. He is leaving for Europe in six weeks. However, he manages to come to our house many times before he leaves. Often he jumps on the trampoline with the boys. He gets me on the trampoline—a rarity. Soon we are all laughing, bouncing, and rolling. I haven't had this much fun in a very long time.

When I ask Alito to tell me what kinds of activities I could do to help Nicky, he says simply, "Play with him, jump on the tramp. I can't think of anything better for him than that."

He gives Nicky a rare gift when he comes to play. He meets him completely at his level, without agendas. As they wrestle around, I remember when I used to heap teddy bears on Nicky when he was little. We called it "wrestling bears," and it was one of the first "games" we played. It occurs to me that I could allow more time to just get silly. I've forgotten somewhere along the way, amidst all the intensive "interventions" and "treatments," that play is just as important as anything else in life.

Funny how someone can fall into your life when you least expect it, split you open, and show you that what you're missing is already inside you. That rare and special person who, by example, teaches you how to let go and have fun. Alito dropped into our lives like an angel of joy. He still bounces back in occasionally, to check up on us.

Chapter 7

"Most of the shadows in this life are caused by standing in one's own sunshine." (Ralph Waldo Emerson)

Nicky at Nine

His hands hold tightly to the chains on the swing in our backyard. Feet, clad in black rubber boots, almost drag in the mud where the grass has worn away.

"Swing me, Mom, higher."

"OK, one more time." I heave. He is nine years old. Getting heavier and heavier to push.

"Up, up, higher! How about another underdog?"

"One more underdog," I say firmly. With a running start, my hands grab the bottom of the swing. I run underneath him, pushing him out and over my head. Simultaneously we both say, "Underdog, da da da Dump de da!!!"

His face reads pure happiness. His eyes are closed as he feels the wind and the pull of gravity. Swinging balances and calms him. It soothes the part of me that aches to share easy times with him.

The momentum from the underdog lasts about a minute and he comes to a standstill.

"Just a little more pushing?" he pleads.

I want him to learn to use his own muscles, his own momentum. A mother can only push for so long, and then she pushes her baby out of the nest. We have been working on swinging for almost four years. I never realized that swinging was a complicated body move until I tried to teach my child, who can't seem to couple coordination and strength.

"Try to make yourself go, Nicky," I encourage him. "Back and forth, legs straight, and bend—forward and back."

"But I can't! It's too hard," he protests, wiggling in pretend agony in the swing. He twists the chains of the swing around and around and snaps free in a spin. Sometimes I regret teaching him this trick.

"I will give you another underdog if you will try," I bribe.

"Oh, all right."

The superhero on the swing takes off with much

fanfare. My own momentum carries me away from the swing set towards the clothesline. My back is still turned as I pull the towels off the line.

"There's no need to fear. Underdog is here!" His voice causes me to turn. I see black boots pushing against a blue sky and an L-shaped body bending, straight, and back. I can't believe what I see and almost drop the laundry. He is swinging all by himself. Here we are on a day like any other, and everything falls into place.

"I'm doing it, Mom, I'm flying solo."

I stand there staring at my Underdog, who is taking off on his own.

Unfortunately, the passengers on Flight 582 are served chicken Parmesan for lunch. Nicky can't stand the smell of cheese, and having nowhere to run, he dives down onto the floor of the cramped plane, gagging. The only thing I can think of to do is to give him a square of chocolate to hold against his nose. But he is a kid and he eats it. I remember a small vial of cologne in my purse. I douse a napkin with it and give it to Nicky to hold under his nose.

I eat pretzels. Ben moves to the back of the plane for lunch.

Nicky is tired, so tired. He looks quite pale, as he sometimes does. After a two-hour drive to the airport and five hours on the plane, we are all in pathetic shape. "It's worth it," I say to myself, "for them to get to know their great-grandfather."

My grandfather greets us at the tiny Texas airport. He is a wizened, wiry, and very active eighty-five year old. His face is carved in deep lines from years and years of hard outdoor work. My aunt, who lives near my grandfather, and my mother, who has flown in from Florida, are waiting for us back at his house. Papa Mac gives me a strong hug and a deep laugh. He bends down to hug the boys. He insists on carrying as many suitcases as humanly possible and leads the way to his truck.

We drive past mesquite trees and a barn that has "Jesus Saves" painted on its side. It is not pretty country, just miles and miles of flatlands. But the sun is setting, and vivid colors vibrate up the enormous sky.

Finally, we arrive at Papa Mac's house. Spec and Pancho, his lap dogs, yap at us strangers. The barking of the dogs sends Nicky's hands up to his ears. He finds the noise intolerable and yells loudly, "Those dogs are bothering me. Make those dogs be quiet!" He barks back at them.

My grandfather, who is almost deaf, says sternly, "Those dogs are just excited. Don't worry about it." But Nicky is worried, and it is causing him discomfort. "Now you put those dogs outside, Daddy," says my aunt. Not wanting to start the visit off tensely, I decide to take the boys for a walk down to the lake nearby.

Nicky is very happy to throw rocks into the muddy water. Ben is on the lookout for water moccasins. I sit and listen to the mourning doves and can't believe how hot it is, even at dusk. We stay down at the lake for as long as possible.

When we get back, supper is about ready. Of course, nothing that Nicky will eat is being served. My grandfather makes a comment about children eating what is placed in front of them. My mom graciously digs a can of Spaghetti-Os out of the pantry. For a little while, everything is OK. Then the dogs start barking again and all hell breaks loose. I take Nicky and Ben to the department store down the road.

We take our time cruising the aisles. I buy several

easy puzzles, plastic army men, and Leggos. Christmas in June. We definitely need to keep busy. We stop off at the drive-in for milkshakes. I think we will survive Day One.

The next morning Nicky is agitated because he is in an unfamiliar environment. It is routine and sameness that make the world tolerable for him.

"When are we going to go home, Mom?" he asks about twenty times in rapid succession. He continues, "It is selfish for us to stay in Texas when our home is in Oregon."

I tell him we will leave Monday morning, and show him on the calendar. He falls on the floor on the verge of a tantrum. I am not sympathetic even though I understand the problem. I know he is very anxious and that the change in routine is hard for him. But sometimes I find myself resenting his rigidity, and then I feel ashamed of myself for it. I feel myself riding downward on an emotional escalator.

"Let's go throw some rocks in the lake," I say.

We take another walk down to the lake. My grandfather joins us. As the boys run ahead, he asks me questions about autism. I can see that he doesn't "get" it. To him, people who are disabled have to look that way. He just shakes his head from side to side.

That afternoon we all go downtown to the annual town bash—the "Whoop-de-do." "We timed this just right," I say to my mom. "This has got to be the most exciting thing that happens here all year." Ben is excited to see the cowboys and floats, but Nicky is scared and wound up. Something snaps in him. He breaks free of my hand and takes off, chasing one of the parade floats. My grandfather and I chase after him.

When we catch him, my grandfather is really angry. He has never seen a child "behave" so badly. "There's nothing wrong with this boy," he says over and over. "He just won't mind." I try to explain but find myself too exhausted to be clear. Nicky promises not to run away again.

Eventually we find my mom and Ben at the street fair. Both of the boys have a great time playing games where everyone wins. We share cotton candy and lemonade. All is not lost. We just need to carry on.

That evening, after I put the kids to bed, my grandfather starts in again about how there is nothing wrong with my son. I could easily get very hot and argue with him. Instead of letting it get to me, I begin to plan tomorrow's activities out loud. He won't understand autism in a weekend. Besides, earlier that day my aunt summed up the situation, "Don't worry about him. This is the man who doesn't believe in germs because he can't see them."

Mother is seething. "Don't sweat it," I whisper to her on my way to the bedroom. Yet I hear her, hot under the collar, trying to educate him, trying to make him understand.

I lie on the bed and remember when I was a child. My grandfather patiently hid peanuts under his gnarled hands and pretended to sleep while we "stole" them. He taught me how to sharpen a pocket knife and ride a horse. Later, when I was a teen, he gave me driving lessons in the pasture in his old Ford Falcon. He was a steady force and he loved me.

Some days I feel I can take on the whole world and help them understand the truth about this bewildering disorder that affects my son. But I cannot bear to argue with this old man I've loved so long. In the face of ignorance, I surrender.

A well worn yet invisible path exists in my neighborhood. Nicky and I begin by making a right turn and heading up the street, a small incline, then turn left on a gravel road.

"Look, it's the log house," he says with the same amazement and excitement he exhibited four years ago when he first laid eyes on it. A friend of mine once said, "Unlike most other people, Nicky gets excited by the familiar." He then runs down the road and lies down on the sidewalk, which never fails to annoy me, and waits for me to catch up.

As we turn the corner he stoops to pick up a handful of pine needles. He tells me they are pine needles. Always. We round the corner with no particular topic, but he has an agenda.

There is a low brick retaining wall that he likes to walk on as if it were a balance beam. First he walks away from the street and then backtracks. Then he follows me along the sidewalk, parallel to the street, until the bricks run out. His sense of balance is amazing.

"Believing I had supernatural powers, I slammed into a brick wall," he quotes, from Paul Simon's *Graceland* album. He loves this album and especially likes the song "Boy in a Bubble." I have always thought this uncanny. He knows the entire album word for word, note for note, beat for beat, and has since he was four years old.

We hit the home stretch. He points to a giant fir tree and tells me it is very big. His love of trees fascinates me. We also have a familiar bike route, and when I once suggested we try a new route he protested vehemently. I finally uncovered the reason: "I will miss the cedar trees," he said. I had never noticed them, but there they were—a tall stand of about twelve cedar trees on an otherwise stark bike path. Of course, they were planted in a neat line.

Our walk is almost over. He shows me the "sticky pitch" of the cedar tree across from our house. I humor him as best I can. For me, it is hard, if not impossible, to be fascinated by the familiar, although to some degree we all crave the comfort of well-worn patterns. At least the seasons change, bringing small but new sights—sparrows splashing in the gutter on an April morning, purple camas flowers growing near the log house in June, leaves rustling in September, a bird's nest exposed against a sharp blue January sky.

I must hold him from behind, with his arms crossed in front of his small chest like a straight jacket. I cannot let go, for if I do, he might lash out at me with his hands, clawed like a tiger's, and strike an angry red line across my face.

We struggle on the floor, my back to the door. I try to keep him from wiggling out from under me by putting the weight of my legs over his and squeezing ever tighter.

He has been screaming for thirty minutes. He is like a fire alarm that sounds without warning, and I am struggling to put out the fire. For years, it has been hard to determine how such blazes begin . . . perhaps some small change in his routine, or a desire that cannot be fulfilled. Whatever it is, I'll have to piece it together later.

My words are low and comforting. I must breathe out the tension that I feel inside and not let my desperation overwhelm me—for what good would that do in the end? We must both get through this rage and find safer feelings.

"Take a deep breath, like Mom. Breathe, Nicky." He continues to thrash, butts his head backwards into my chest, and knocks the wind out of me. Words of comfort or reason simply do not get through, and so I begin to chant "OHM," a calming mantra I learned in yoga class. I can think of nothing else to do but bring this ancient sound forward in the hope that what has been uttered for centuries to produce calm and clarity for meditators will have some effect on my child. "OOOHHHMMM. . . ." By the sixth repetition he begins to relax a little.

"Take a deep breath with Mommy," I repeat to him. The struggling ceases, and he takes a tiny breath. A quick involuntary gasp for air follows, the kind that occurs after one has been crying nonstop for a long time. We breathe together slowly. His body softly collapses against mine. I loosen my arms and simply rock him back and forth.

"It's OK now," I tell him. "You're OK."

He looks at me. All the rage is gone. His eyes have been washed a brighter blue from the tears.

"I'm OK now. Nicky's OK."

I walk out of the church in the small town where I was born. The afternoon sun envelops me, and within seconds my blouse is clinging to my back. I tell my brother and sister that I need a few minutes alone, before we go to my cousin's house to prepare for my father's wake.

In the courtyard, I sit on a smooth concrete bench under the shade of magnolias and redbud trees. A blue jay squawks overhead, chasing a mockingbird away into the quiet blue sky.

A week ago I sent Dad a Father's Day card—three weeks before Father's Day. I had not spoken to him for years. The card didn't say much, really. "Hi, Dad. Happy Father's Day. We went fishing last weekend. I know how much you like to fish. Are you catching anything in Lake Travis? Even though we haven't spoken in a long time, know that I love you." Sending the card didn't make any sense to me at the time, but then, nothing about our relationship ever did.

Ironically, Dad had a "thing" about Father's Day. Over the years he always expressed his disappointment if I neglected to send a card acknowledging his paternity. He was a man who could never be much of a father, largely because of his addiction to alcohol and whatever other demons tortured him. Mother left him when I was five. Twenty years of occasional visits had only produced bizarre, regrettable scenes.

The last straw came years ago, when I took Nicky to visit my grandparents. I was so proud of my new baby, my new life. Why was I surprised when Dad showed up at my grandmother's house already drunk? He made off with my husband for hours, drinking all the while. They finally returned after midnight, Dad reeling and quoting the Bible, Rand pale and unnerved. Why on earth did I expect anything different? We left that night. Except for this Father's Day card, that had been my last attempt to continue a relationship that had filled me with sadness and regret.

Three days ago a series of strokes sent Dad into a coma. His body was badly worn from cirrhosis and the onset of cancer. The doctor advised us that the strokes had damaged his brain, and even if heroic measures could save him, the probability was high that he would be blind and paralyzed for the rest of his life. My brother, sister, and I were given the responsibility of choosing to continue or to remove the life-support system. None of us could visualize such a future for him, the man who lived to party and golf. Over the phone, we agonized about this terrible decision for half the night, searching our hearts for compassion and truth. We finally felt we knew what he would want. He died when I was in flight, on my way to say goodbye.

An hour ago, in the church, one question burned inside me, and only one answer could give me peace. I sought out the woman I'd never met, Dad's latest girlfriend—hoping she would know.

"Did he . . . did he get the card I sent?"

"Yes, Honey, he did, the day before the stroke. It meant a lot to him."

Finally, something has made sense.

The blue jay returns and splashes in the nearby birdbath. My brother and sister come and sit on either side of me. Hidden in the canopy of leaves above, a mockingbird trills its evening song.

Chapter 8

"Compassion is like sunlight, awakening and bringing joy to beings. Its beauty is like a rainbow, lifting the hearts of all who see it." (Tarthang Tulku)

Here I am, on the last leg of my journey home. I boarded my first plane in North Carolina, the country's last "smoking encouraged" airport, bound for Oregon (where all smokers will be deported). I am embarking on the final, forty-minute shuttle flight home.

It has been a long week for me, selling my book at an autism conference. Parents come up and talk about their children, desperate for answers. Usually I can only offer them empathy or pass on a trick that has worked for me. There are no easy answers.

At conferences I see a steady stream of humanity flowing past my booth, children and adults with a wide range of severity of symptoms. One man with autism came up to me and said, "Can I have a hug? Hugs are something I never get." We hugged, and then he gathered his book bag and walked on. Every time I attend a conference I am reminded that there are so many children and adults in the world—thousands and thousands of them—that need acceptance and compassion.

Worn out, I toss my purse under the seat and look absently out the window onto the dark tarmac. Last to board, a woman and a girl of about ten struggle to get into the small, crowded plane. The girl flaps her hand frantically near her face. The pair move in a sort of lunging, shuffling duet. The mother's eyes are firmly fixed toward the rear of the plane and her hand is vise-gripped to the girl's wrist. I know this scenario: mother and child with autism traveling. Small world.

Loud guttural sounds, almost a moan, almost a scream, come from the girl. Her first utterance causes the people near me to shift around in their seats and nervously clear their throats.

I glance back. The mother is working overtime to get her daughter to settle down and stay calm as we take off and gain altitude. It is hard for anyone to stay calm on a little airplane. I look down as the brightly lit buildings of Portland give way to the faint lights of small towns and farms.

The girl's sounds begin to escalate as the plane hits some turbulence. Fellow passengers murmur. To me, of course, this feels like home. I've just spent a week surrounded by children with this disability and I'm going home to Nicky.

More NOISE. The child is obviously upset and uncomfortable. At least that's obvious to me. The pressure in her ears is probably giving her excruciating pain. I am jarred from my internal reflection by a man's cold remark.

"Why can't she make her be quiet?" the passenger behind me complains loudly.

"Why the hell did she bring her on a plane," hisses the other. Passengers in the seats next to them chuckle.

It's all I can do not to turn around and shout, "Be glad that you aren't that uncomfortable. Be glad that you aren't that child's caretaker, having to dread taking a short, forty minute flight because of cutting remarks from jerks like you. Aren't you glad she isn't your child because if she was you couldn't just get off a plane and walk away from her!" But I stew in silence.

The plane is descending. We will touch ground soon. The people behind me will get off the plane and glide down to their baggage and their cars. Perhaps they will stop for a martini before they go home, with only themselves to worry about.

The mother in the rear of the plane will wait until everyone else is off, struggle down the rickety steps, carrying too many bags and trying to keep a grip on a tired, crotchety girl. A week from now the others will not even remember this flight or the girl who was making so much noise. I will not be able to forget her.

The sun is shining through the enormous window panes of the optical shop and glances off the rows and rows of glasses. A woman flings the entry door wide open and steps inside, deftly holding the door with one foot while her arm helps a teenage girl over the threshold. The girl smiles widely, and saliva spills from the side of her mouth. She lets out a loud sound: "EEIIGLA!" "EEIIGLAAA!"

The woman's eyes quickly scan the room until she finds two empty chairs. "That's right, we're here to get you new eyeglasses," the woman says, pushing her graying brown hair behind her ears. Waiting customers look up, then quickly back down to their outdated magazines.

Once the girl is seated, the woman goes over to the counter, standing sideways to keep an eye on her while she talks to the receptionist. This takes less than a minute. Then she is back to the girl, who has gotten up and is wandering in slow, jerky movements over to one of the display cases. "EEIIGLA." A hand twists into the air, aiming at the rows of waiting glasses.

"Yes, we will choose some for you as soon as it is our turn," the caregiver says as she carefully guides the girl back to her chair. The eyeglasses the girl is wearing are held together at the sides with a piece of masking tape.

The woman adjusts her large flowered overshirt and composes herself briefly. Then she pulls a series of books from her worn canvas bag. They are children's books. The girl listens and points intently to the colorful pictures as the woman softly reads them to her. Glancing at the clock frequently, the woman removes one book after the other—*Hop on Pop, The*

Little Engine That Could, The Cat in the Hat—working hard to keep the girl occupied.

It is a well-orchestrated succession, timed impeccably, one book following the other. The woman does not even put the finished books down. She puts them between her knees and holds them there, seemingly unaware that her legs are visibly shaking.

I reach over and gently pull the books from her pressed knees and place them on the chair next to her. At first she is startled, but then she breaks out into a big smile and says, "Thanks." Before I can respond, the lab tech calls my name and waves my glasses in the air. They have moved on to another book anyway.

I drive to Portland to visit a family that has traveled from Korea to find treatments for their son, Anand. This will be my second visit with this family, and I am very much looking forward to seeing them again. Over a year has passed since we first met.

I recall with fondness the first time I heard Vrinda's soft voice over the phone: "I got your number from Dr. Edelson. He gave me your book. It has been tremendously helpful. Already we have flown to New York and had an appointment with an eye specialist listed there. Our son is newly diagnosed and we need to know as much as we can about autism. We would like to meet you."

As I look back, I am embarrassed at my initial reaction. "Most of the information you need is there in the book. The decisions you make are up to you. Hopefully, you will make a lot of phone calls while you are here in the States. I really don't know what else I can tell you." In other words, don't bother me further.

"No, really. We won't take up much of your time. Just ask a few questions. There is so little information in Korea. We could take a taxi to Eugene."

That did it. A two-hour taxi ride! How could I say no to this persistent, soft-spoken woman of steel? I agree to meet them halfway in two days.

There are bright piñatas inside the Mexican restaurant, paper palm trees, and blinking neon signs for Corona beer. I wonder if it is going to be possible to keep a child with autism and his three-year-old sister quiet in this visually stimulating place.

I order a soft drink and begin eating corn chips.

When the basket of chips is nearly empty and I have glanced at my watch about twenty times, I begin to grow restless and impatient. Then the waitress comes to me with a message.

"Your friends' cab got a flat tire, but they should be here soon." Suddenly, I feel ashamed. Here is a family from out of the country, with two small children, one severely disabled. I visualize them standing by the side of the freeway with two cranky kids and probably worried that they are late. I have it easy, sitting in a nice air-conditioned restaurant, quiet and alone. I order another pop.

About fifteen minutes later, a tired looking couple with children enters the restaurant, glancing anxiously around. I wave to them and they settle into the booth. When Vrinda's big brown eyes meet mine, I feel a rush of compassion. Until then, I had felt that meeting them was a burden. I receive many phone calls from frustrated parents of children with autism. All of them are justifiably angry, sad, or depressed. One caller said that she was at her wits' end, that she had considered shooting her son to end their misery! These calls never fail to break my heart. They send me crying to God, "Why?"

We talk for over an hour. Vrinda is hungry, but

not for food. My enchiladas grow cold as I do my best to answer each of her questions. Anand, sitting next to me, occasionally reaches over to my plate and takes a chip. His father, Ravi, tries to stop him, but right away I say, "Let him eat from my plate. I don't mind, and that way we can talk." I hope that maybe Anand will sense that I am a friend. Vrinda wants to know every single thing I know about autism. I recognize this hunger, this insatiable desire to know what can be done to help one's child. Ravi patiently shows the children around the restaurant to keep them occupied.

Vrinda tells me about her home in Korea and about India, where they were born and raised. She describes how in India, disability rights are far behind what they are in the US and says that information is at a premium. She buys five extra copies of my book to take home with her.

When it comes time to say goodbye, Vrinda pulls out a small box. "I bought this in New York for you because without your book I would not have known where to go for help." Inside was a beautiful pin. Two brushed gold loops circle a third one that is heavily encrusted with brilliant rhinestones. I turn it over in my hand and then put it on.

"It is like our lives, Vrinda. Our children link us together." She smiles in agreement.

Now, over a year later, I am going back to see them. The drive to Portland is a joy for me, an honor. I pull into the parking lot of a modest motel. For two weeks this family of four has been crammed into a small room with a kitchenette. Yet Vrinda is calm and gracious. Anand, his sister, Indu, and I bounce together on the bed. He is older and is doing better. He is more verbal, and he looks at me much more than he did during their last visit. Vrinda has worked with him intensively for twenty to thirty hours a week. She tells me that sometimes she is at the brink of exhaustion but feels that it is her duty. I assure her that the effort is paying off.

We drive to a physical therapy office, where Anand receives cranial-sacral treatment and sensory integration therapy. In a small room, the therapist manipulates Anand's muscular tissues. He lets out an ear-piercing scream, as if in intense pain. Tears come to my eyes, but I resist the urge to stop her. Within a few minutes Anand seems calmer and more relaxed. He puts his head in the therapist's lap, resting like this for several minutes. Later, I ask Vrinda about

116

his cry. She tells me that she too wanted to stop the therapist at first, but feels Anand shows improvement afterwards and that she has learned to accept his initial discomfort.

On the drive back to the hotel room, Anand is quiet, almost subdued. Indu looks tired. How hard it must be on this little girl to attend these daily procedures in a strange country, so far from home. How hard on all of them. Yet they never complain, not once. They focus on their gratitude—that they can afford to do this financially and, most importantly, that Anand is responding positively.

I have brought books to donate to Vrinda's cause of providing information about autism in India. It seems like such a small offering. Anand, Indu, and I bounce a little more on the bed. Vrinda serves me some delicious Indian spinach soup, and I ask her for the recipe.

Soon I must leave. I tell Anand goodbye. His eyes lock with mine for an instant. He says, "Bye." Vrinda asks him to give me a kiss. I lean over to get one, and he draws close. Suddenly, he opens his mouth and tries to take a bite out of my cheek! My hand is quick and stops him short.

"Anand!" Vrinda looks mortified.

"Vrinda, it was only a love nip," I joke. "He said goodbye and looked at me." I give her a long hug. Who knows if we'll ever see each other again.

On the way home I have to pull off the road and sob. I think of all the Anands in the world, I multiply them times two . . . their parents. I feel all their love, sorrow, and suffering. There is so much work to be done. I touch the pin on my coat, the one Vrinda gave me a year ago, take a deep breath, and drive on.

On a cold February morning, I receive a letter and poems from a man living in a foreign country. The carefully handwritten, three-page letter describes a life of endurance and survival in a world that insults his senses.

"I am sixty-four years of age and live alone with two cats, spending most of my time in bed loaded with five heavy wool blankets, with the two cats on top. In this way I get some relief from the sensory-overload bombardment, which I am unable to filter very well (light and noise)."

He further writes that he has gotten no relief from medication or psychologists with "psychodynamic agendas," but has been helped somewhat by reading books by individuals who also suffer from autism.

Linguistically fluent, he states, "I am perhaps a minor verbal savant, inasmuch as I can produce grammatical utterances of no practical value in several languages." He was not able to finish his graduate studies in linguistics, citing his inability to write a thesis or to survive in the social environment of school. He did, however, teach himself expressive intonation by studying Chinese.

Finally, he states, "The clinicians I have seen, quite simply take my linguistic fluency to be communica-tion—which I know it is not. Communication is not just well-formed sentences. It is also, and perhaps primarily, intentionality, meaning in context, power negotiation. All my interaction with people has been in terms of my submission to their agendas. I have never been able to participate in a group conversation because I simply don't understand what is going on in the nonverbal or 'protolinguistic' domain. I have never in my life addressed anyone who grasped the nature of my confusion and disorientation. Are you possibly the person who does understand?"

I read the letter many times, read the poems filled with feelings of longing and isolation. Tears well and spill over as I visualize his life, this man alone with his two cats. If I am one who understands, it is because he has, through this letter, achieved what he so eloquently describes as his lifelong struggle. He has communicated with me, and his message pierces the deepest place in my heart.

I pick up my pen, hoping I can give as much.

I step into the toy store at the mall to say hello to my friend Peggy, who works there. Peggy has a boy with autism too, about Nicky's age, and we are part of a group that advocates for children with disabilities. She is ready to take a break, so we go get frozen yogurt and take it over to the bench in the middle of the mall.

A man is walking towards us. I would have to say he looks a bit "odd." Maybe it is his clothes, or is it the way he is clutching his out-of-place briefcase so tightly to his chest? He seems very pale, even from here.

"Oh no," says Peggy, "it's Jim."

"Who's Jim?" I ask.

"He's always, always at the mall. He goes around showing everybody his picture of his dead mother, business cards that he has collected, and his bottle cap collection. He is sweet but, well, sometimes. . . ."

"Sounds like autism," I start in, but I stop because Jim has now made it to where we are and sits on other side of the bench. Peggy and I face each other, knees almost knocking, our backs to him. For a moment, we freeze harder than the yogurt.

I peek behind me. He has removed his bottle cap collection from the briefcase and is carefully lining up the caps on the bench.

Peggy and I stare at each other. We share the same thought: this man could be our children grown. Will people snicker at them, turn their backs to them on such a bench? We are uncomfortable with Jim because we don't want to look ahead to when our children are his age.

Right now, both Peggy and I are averting our attention from Jim, and I think how strange and silly it is to be avoiding someone who probably shares the same disability as our children. If we are this uncomfortable, then how must other people (who don't know anything about autism) feel when Jim sits next to them on a bench?

Jim is not "bothering" us. He is not trying to start a conversation or engage our interest. Peggy and I take a few more bites of yogurt. Is she feeling as hypocritical as I? Yes. A moment later she sighs and rolls her eyes at me and then nods toward Jim. We slowly turn to face him, and smile.

"Hi, Jim," says Peggy, "where did you get all those bottle caps?"

Chapter 9

There are plants and animals that live so far down under the sea, beyond sunlight, that they create their own light through an internal chemical synthesis. A parent of a child with autism once said to me, "Nobody knows the way we live. Sometimes it feels as though we are inhabiting the same planet but in another dimension—perhaps somewhere just this side of normal."

Nicky at Eleven

Nicky and I hike up the Butte just outside the city limits. As with so many of our familiar activities, his stops are predictable.

"Be careful of rattlesnakes," he says, pausing and pointing to the warning notice on the brown Forest Service sign nailed high on a Douglas fir.

"I will, Nicky," I reply seriously. Last year he learned to read, and when he first read this sign he marched decidedly back to the car and refused to hike up the Butte for a year for fear of rattlers. With a year of steady information about rattlesnakes and hearing the statement over and over that snakes are generally afraid of people, Nicky has become convinced that if he stays on the trail, his chances of suffering snakebite are minimal compared to the fun of the hike.

The sheltering columns of pine and fir create a dark and hushed world. We hike past the long-dead tree, shaped like a dragon, nose pointing towards the summit. Turning at the switchback on the dark north side, we pretend trolls live under the mossy boulders there. Nicky leads the way. He likes to be the "leader" on most outings. His uncanny, map-like memory never fails, and he navigates us along the most direct route to the top.

I recall a hike six years ago, when Nicky was only five. Halfway up the trail he turned and ran screaming all the way down to the car. Running pell-mell after him, I caught up with him in the parking lot.

"My head might get stuck in the clouds, Mom," he repeated over and over, refusing to rejoin our party on the trail. This phobia kept him on low ground for the rest of that summer.

At the top there are outcrops of smooth rock to sit on, where we rest and admire the panoramic view of the valley. Each of the four directions holds a special point of interest for Nicky.

"Portland is to the north, Mom, 105 miles away. To the east are the snow-capped mountains. To the south is California, where my grandparents live. And to the west is the beach where I like to go and splash in the waves."

He must tell me these things. Facts are comforting and easily verbalized. He relaxes for a few minutes, chewing on a chocolate-chip granola bar. A buzzard circles below us. I lean back on the warm rock to soak in the sun.

"Mom, it's time to go."

"We just got here, Nicky."

"But I'm feeling nervous."

"Why?" I look at him and see that he is a bit pale.

"Well, it's just that my head might get stuck in the clouds. It's time to go."

"Come on," I say, "you know that isn't going to happen. How about a few more minutes?" I bargain.

He agrees, fidgets, sighs, and lies face down on the rock.

As we begin the hike down, his step is urgent, his face looks furtively upwards at times. At the bottom of the hill he joyfully says, "We made it, my head didn't get stuck in the clouds. Here we are, safe near our car."

Yes, safe. I lean against the nearest tree, catching my breath.

"Be careful mom," Nicky says, pointing upwards: "Beware of rattlesnakes."

Nicky at Twelve

I walk through the door of the florist shop and smell chilled carnations and Victorian potpourri. The memories of choosing football-dance boutonnieres, Mother's Day bouquets, and funeral arrangements all gather together in a cerebral reunion.

Today Nicky turns twelve, and I am here to buy balloons. What's a birthday party without them? If there is a lull and the kids get bored, they can always bounce the balloons around, or pop them, or suck out the helium and imitate squirrels on amphetamines.

I guess I want to guarantee a good time.

Some birthdays have been big productions and they usually end up being a lot of fun. I've been known to invite every child of every friend I have, and every adult I know too. Because I want it to be fun for Nicky. Because he doesn't get invited to many birthday parties.

His birthday sometimes reminds me that he isn't hitting the same milestones as other kids. Every 365 days I wonder how we made it through the last 364. I wonder or worry about the years to come. If history repeats itself during some part of the day, or early the next, I will cry.

I know I'm not alone. Last year my friend told me of a fiasco at her son's birthday. He wanted to go out for pizza with the family. She was relieved. No sweat, no trying to find friends. All was going smoothly until the clown employed by the restaurant came to their table to make him a special animal-shaped balloon. Ironically, her son, John, who has autism, gets sick at the smell of latex balloons and he started to gag. She had to explain the situation to the clown and calm her son, who was moaning under the table. As she told me later, "The clown just kept hovering, not understanding why I wanted him to go away. People at other tables were giving us the 'what kind of mean parents are you?' glances. I wanted to run."

"How can I help you?" How long have I been staring at the wall of balloon choices? "I'm here to get a balloon bouquet for my son," I tell the florist.

"Oh, a boy. How old is he?" she inquires perkily.

"He's. . . ." I flounder, really and truly forgetting for a moment. "He's twelve."

"Oh, well, we have lots to choose from. There's soccer, football, baseball, and hockey motifs. Most boys play at least one of those sports. How about one of those?"

"No, he's not really into sports." (I don't tell her the only flies he catches are the ones with wings. He's good at it, too—he can do it with one hand.) I focus on the balloon with Winnie the Pooh and Piglet. This is the one he would like most of all, I think. I can't think fast enough.

"So, what will it be?" she presses.

I stutter. I almost launch into the truth, telling her that he is twelve, but that socially he is going on seven. He would probably like Pooh the most because half of his language about birthdays comes from the video about Eeyore and his birthday party.

"I'll take the Garfield balloon, and five regular helium balloons too," I say quickly. Am I making myself feel better by making an "age-appropriate" choice? Wishfully growing him up?

"Oh, don't you just love Garfield! Everyone does!" She nods in approval and walks off to prepare my order, unaware of my inner tumult.

On the way home I can't decide whether I'm mad at myself or not. Would he have preferred the Pooh balloon? Was I denying who he is, in some way, to myself? A whole lot of adults like Pooh too. Damn it. I've blown the whole thing out of proportion. I think of John, gagging even at the sight of balloons, and suddenly remember that I've invited him to the party!

I tie the balloons to the chairs around the table. A giant chocolate cake sprinkled with M&Ms sits in the middle. A "Happy Birthday" banner hangs over the doorway. I've called my friend and told her that John should wear a gas mask, and she assures me he'll manage . . . that being invited to a party is what is most important to him. When Nicky arrives home and sees the balloons his face lights up, as it has year after year.

"Garfield!" he exclaims with delight. "He's a mighty silly cat."

Nicky dances in the living room with Carmen Miranda. He is in South America, or South America is in him. Donald Duck, his faithful travel companion, is there too. Jumping off the couch, Nicky's legs move up and down in a crazy chicken dance. His eyes are glassy. He is singing something incomprehensible, with a Spanish accent. He is reliving this scene maybe for the eighty-eighth time with the same exuberance he has had for the last eighty-seven.

Since he received his first video, when he was four years old, the Duck has been like a member of our immediate family. Nicky's first video, *Donald In Mathemagic Land*, was too advanced for him at four years—or so we thought at first. By five, however, Nicky was reciting the information that the Cathedral of Notre Dame had been built using the Pythagorean theorem of the Golden Rectangle.

"Billiards and chess, Mom," he still tells me gravely now and then, "are games of calculated strategy." Wonderful facts, but I still cannot teach him how to play a game of checkers.

I believe he may have watched every Disney cartoon available on video. He is willing to watch others—Max Fleischer, the occasional Tom and Jerry, or Yogi Bear—but nine times out of ten I'd say it is Disney he is watching and, mathematically speaking, the probability that Donald is in one of these is quite high. Many well-meaning people have suggested that I take away the Donald Duck cartoons. Yet for years this was the ONLY guaranteed quiet time I could depend on. He would not move if the Duck was on the screen, getting bonked on the head or chased by a shark. They've flown airplanes, ridden on trains, fought off chipmunks and mountain lions. A friend once came by and remarked that she had never before witnessed such a level of audience participation. The stories are completely part of Nicky's inner world. I do believe I have heard him talking in his sleep about them.

Nicky's ultimate joy is when Ben or I will "act out a Donald." It is a close proximity to imaginative play, and if a casual onlooker came by and saw me charging at him, pretend lance in hand, he would never know that Nicky allows no leeway for interpretation. Follow the video sequence word for word, squawk for squawk, or prepare to face his wrath.

It is funny how I've come to see Donald as one of the most "human" of all the Disney characters. He makes lots of mistakes, and a lot of the cartoons that feature him don't have happy endings, but find him scrapping his way out of a jam.

Over the years I would occasionally ask Nicky why he liked Donald so much. The standard answer was, "Because I do." When he was ten and his expressive language had expanded, he offered this explanation: "I like Donald because he gets mad all the time, gets in trouble for it, and nobody understands his words."

I took a step back. "Do you feel like Donald Duck sometimes?" I asked.

"Yes, for a long time I did. But now, on with the show."

Through the large picture window in our living room I see a squirrel racing around the yard. It shimmies up a young cherry tree and teeters on the thin limbs to reach the fruit. The squirrel holds each cherry in its tiny claws, gnaws the fruit around the pit, discards the seed quickly, and moves on to the next.

Nicky comes into the room and sits down next to me. I point out the squirrel that I've been observing with great delight. Nicky explodes. He sees the squirrel's actions as a threat to a valuable commodity that he has looked forward for a month to having for himself. Before I know it, he is racing out the front door.

"You get out of my cherry tree, you pesky squirrel!" he yells at the top of his lungs. He assumes the persona of Arliss, a little farm boy featured in the movie, *Old Yeller*. Like Arliss in the movie, he picks up some rocks and hurls them at the squirrel.

Now I race out the door. "Nicky, stop throwing rocks at the squirrel! You could hurt it." How many times have I told him, "Try not to hurt any living thing if you can help it"? I want to teach my children about the sanctity of life. I want them to know that all life is precious. Nicky seems to understand the concept for the most part. But I suppose rage has overcome reason.

When he was about six, he brought a dead snake to me and said blankly, "Look, I killed it." That unnerved me. Besides not wanting him to hurt animals, I had suddenly feared that he might hurt another child without being conscious of doing so. It has always been hard to know what connections he is making about cause and effect, and sometimes this scares me most of all.

Many months after the snake incident, when my mother was visiting, she came back into the house after being outside with the boys. She was shaking. "Nicky was holding a snake, Elizabeth! I told him to put it down immediately and never to touch one! What I don't understand is why he kept repeating, 'But I didn't kill it, Grandma, I didn't kill it!' "

How does one draw the line? I swat at flies that get in the house. I learned the hard way that moths in the kitchen aren't cute and left unchecked they will obliterate dry goods within days. And I'm not a vegetarian.

But this moment, near the cherry tree, I want to spare a squirrel a concussion. I repeat to Nicky, "Remember, we do not hurt living things if we can help it. What else could we do?" He is too angry to think and starts yelling at me and the squirrel simultaneously.

"Why don't we give the squirrel something else to eat," I suggest, "so it won't eat your cherries?" He stops yelling and nods. Together we go into the house and scoop up a cupful of black sunflower seeds.

When we return to the yard, we sprinkle them in a pile under the cherry tree.

After we are inside the house for about five minutes, the squirrel returns and stuffs its mouth with seeds. Nicky watches this through the window, smiling. I wonder, has he learned the "larger" lesson, that there are more humane choices than violence? Or, the next time he sees a squirrel stealing cherries, will he simply yell and throw sunflower seeds at it?

A red tulip rests in a vase in the hallway. It has seen better days. One or two curling, brown petals lie next to the vase. On this particular day, I plan to toss it as soon as my cleaning frenzy takes me to that end of the house.

During late afternoon, a shaft of sunlight shoots through the bathroom window and into the usually dark hallway, catching the tulip and illuminating it. I drop the armload of clothes I am carrying and bend down for a closer look. Suddenly, it no longer looks like a flower that needs to be thrown out. It looks like the most beautiful flower I have ever seen. It is like a piece of exquisite Italian hand-blown glass.

The veins on the petals show darkly through a red, glowing velvet fire. It seems to say to me, "Look what light can do. It can change your perspective. There is beauty waiting to be seen, waiting for the light to touch it."

Within a few minutes this moment has passed. One again there is a wilting tulip in a dim hallway. By the next afternoon, the petals have all fallen. But the message keeps blooming.

The sound of the alarm wakes me from the peace of Sunday night's sleep into the "get up and go" of Monday morning. It's nice to have a few minutes of quiet before the demands of the day begin. It is still dark outside, and the boys sleep. Usually, Nicky wakes me up promptly at 6:00 every morning. Today, however, is the first day of their winter break from school, and even Nicky sleeps in.

Half awake, I shuffle from my bedroom to the bathroom, find the cat and toss her outside, then put a kettle of water on the stove. I tiptoe into the boy's room. Ben has kicked off all his covers, and one leg hangs off the bed. Gently I put his leg back on the bed and cover him up. He snuggles deeper into sleep.

I tiptoe to Nicky's bed and bend over to check his alarm in case he forgot it was vacation and set it. I remember the first time he slept through the night, when he was six years old, and what a breakthrough that was. He sleeps with one arm over Red Bear, his dear old friend, one of thirty stuffed animals that cover his bed. At almost thirteen years, some of them remain his best friends.

A glimmer creeps under the window blind. I turn toward the door, hearing the kettle about to whistle. On Nicky's desk, near the door, rests his report card. I glance at it for about the tenth time. This term he ranks straight "A" as a Middle School student. But what amazes me the most are his teachers' comments: "Has positive attitude"; "Excellent work habits"; "Pleasure to have in class."

I feel extraordinary gratitude toward the progressive administrator in our district who hired Cyndi, Nicky's aide. For the last three years she has sat near him in class, keeping him focused, helping him interpret the world of expectations. Without her support, her ingenuity, her ability to teach, Nicky might still be a "nonreader." He might still be spinning down the sidewalk. We have been helped in our struggle by so many wonderful people. There are thousands of children and adults with autism who, like Nicky, need the patience, the compassion, the heart-felt giving of others.

He has come far. Yet the inconsistencies of autism remain. One minute he pretends to be a cartoon, and then the next he might carefully turn off a radio news program concerning war (which a "normal" child might not even comprehend) and say quietly, "This is too upsetting."

Only the other day I reprimanded him for using bad table manners and he blew up and stormed out of the room. Later he came back to apologize, but he blamed it on the pancakes. "Those darn pancakes! They caused me to use bad manners. I'll never eat them again!" Tomorrow anything could happen—a temper could snap, a seizure could occur, and gains could be lost. We have yet to make it through the perils of adolescence. We who know Nicky well have learned to live moment to moment.

I turn and look back at my sleeping sons. I wouldn't, couldn't, have imagined the complexities of mothering a child with autism—the struggles, the heartaches, and the opportunities to learn and love. Once these boys were only the dream of a girl who wanted to be a mother. Now, they are two living "wishes come true," with wishes of their own. What new dreams and possibilities are yet to be for them? For me? I return to the kitchen and reach the kettle before it cries.

I glance at the wall calendar that hangs near the stove. I notice two small words in the square that marks today: Winter Solstice—the shortest day of the year. Tomorrow, the light will begin to increase gradually, a little bit each day. Ever circling the sun, the earth and everyone on it . . . spinning.

9 781932 565034